IN THE
BEGINNING

IN THE BEGINNING

Stories from the Bible

Sholem Asch

Translated by
CAROLINE CUNNINGHAM

Drawings by ELEANOR KLEMM

SCHOCKEN BOOKS • NEW YORK

First SCHOCKEN edition 1966

Copyright 1935 by Sholem Asch

Library of Congress Catalog Card No. 66-24907

Manufactured in the United States of America

10 9 8 7 6 5 4 3 2   78 79 80 81

CONTENTS

IN THE
BEGINNING

ADAM

God had already made heaven and earth, every kind of grass and herb, fruitful trees and plants in the forest, birds flying in the sky, wild beasts and cattle, and everything that creeps upon the earth; but no one was yet there to be the ruler. There were no buildings on the earth; the cattle ate the grass, but the fruit on the trees and the wheat in the fields were still untouched. Among the animals, however, there was no order and no harmony; and often when they came together to consider some serious matter, they would at once begin making a great uproar, fighting, and beating one another; they grew mad with rage and wild; they did not understand one another and did not know what they should talk about. The small animals were too timid, the wild ones too powerful; the birds squeaked dreadfully and flew backward and forward over the dignified heads of the lions and bears who had gathered together in the woods for counsel.

So God saw that the animals could not rule the world, and He created man to govern them, and to look after everything. All things were to belong to him: the fish in the sea, the beasts in the forest, the birds in the air, and everything that lived in the great world. And God took a piece of earth and formed a man out of it. He breathed the breath of life into him so that he became a living soul, and could see, hear, walk about, and understand everything. And God ordered all the creatures that lived upon the earth to march in front of the man so that they should know their master, and that the man might give names to them. And God said to Adam:

"All the creatures in the world I have made for you; and the names you give to them now, they will keep for all time."

Then the man sat down upon a hill and the animals marched past him.

At first heavy steps were heard as the enormous elephant came along, and when Adam saw him he said:

"He has a long nose like an elephant, so he shall be called Elephant—and he was at once so named. Then came the lion, proud as a king, shaking his mane and roaring so loud that everything around began to tremble. Then the man said:

"He roars exactly like a lion, so I will call him Lion"—and he was promptly given that name. Then the horse came galloping along. He snorted through his nostrils and neighed. And Adam said:

"He neighs and jumps just like a horse, so he shall

be called Horse"—and thus he was named immediately.

So God led every living animal before Adam, and Adam gave names to all of them which they have kept to this very day.

EVE

But Adam was very sad and anxious because he was obliged to live utterly alone. The longing for a human being became so strong within him that he could no longer bear it. So he arose and set out into the wide world to search for a creature who would be exactly like himself. He walked and walked, wandering day and night over hill and valley, but he could not find a man; only wild animals, cattle and birds met him on his journey.

After he had thus wandered around the world for a long while and had not found any one, he felt such deep misery in his loneliness that he was willing to make friends with the animals.

But the lion and the bear did not please him because they were so terribly bad and he was afraid of learning to be bad from them. The ox and the cow were however too dumb and he could not talk with them at all. The horse and the dog he liked the best of all, for they were faithful friends and could be depended upon. And so they became good companions. But friendship with the animals did not last long; he could never speak a thoughtful word with them, or sit at a meal, for they were so dirty and did not have polite manners at the table or in company.

So Adam grew more sorrowful and his longing for a human being became still greater. It happened one day that he came to a large pool of water; he bent down over it and discovered on the surface a creature which he had never met before in the whole world. Adam was very much surprised at this and called to the creature:

"Come out here to me!"

But it did not come out. It beckoned to him in just the same way that he did, and his words also came back to him, only he did not know where they came from.

And Adam grew sad at heart; he went away from the water's edge, sank down on a hill-side and fell into a deep sleep.

But the Lord saw how deeply Adam grieved in his loneliness and had pity upon him. He came down from heaven, took a rib from his side and made a woman out of it. He breathed a soul into her and soon after she became alive. Then He healed up Adam's side so that nothing at all could be noticed. When Adam awakened, a woman lay beside him. He was greatly pleased, and spoke to her saying:

"Who are you? Where do you come from?"

Then the woman said:

"I do not know."

"Did you come to me out of the water?" Adam asked again.

"I do not know," answered the woman. "As I opened my eyes, I was lying beside you."

When Adam heard this, he took her by the hand and went with her to the pool of water in which he had seen the strange creature; and this time the mirror showed him two people, for the man in the water had also got a woman. Adam was greatly astonished at this, but he nevertheless was heartily pleased with his own wife; he took her by the hand and went with her through the wide world.

PARADISE GARDEN

Adam and Eve lived in Paradise Garden. What a glorious garden it was! Never was there a lovelier one in the whole big world. The Lord had planted in it all kinds of beautiful trees and wondrous rare flowers of splendid colors; they never faded, and always gave out a sweet perfume. The finest fruits hung on the trees in abundance. And every day there was nice crisp bread and rolls. But nobody needed first to sow the seed, till the soil, grind the grain, stir the meal, or bake the loaf. In the Garden of Paradise the earth yielded bread without sowing the seed and without ploughing the field. The wine did not come, as it does today, from grapes; it was offered ready-made in cups of red rose-leaves. The birds were dressed in the gayest feathers, they flew back and forth and filled the air with the sweetest melodies. There was never any night in Paradise or any winter; the sun shone continually and was very warm and bright yet never too hot, because a gentle wind blew all the time; it was very mild and pleasant and cooled the hot rays of the sun.

In the beautiful garden Adam and Eve wandered around naked, and were not ashamed before each other. Everything belonged to them and was their own property. If they were thirsty they needed only to call. Almost immediately two doves would whir down to earth and hold out to them in their little beaks rose-cups filled with wine. If they wanted to have a nice ride, they needed only to beckon and two eagles at once came flying down on their great wings. Then Adam and Eve would sit on their backs and fly off like the birds in the air, amusing themselves as long as they liked. But if on their wanderings they came to a large sheet of water and could go no farther, they needed merely to signal with their hands and two whales came up out of the waves. Adam and Eve would sit on their backs and swim across.

In the midst of the Garden of Paradise, among many other trees stood one which was called the tree of life. Whoever ate of its fruit lived forever. And another tree was standing there which was called the tree of knowledge. Whoever ate of its fruit, became all at once very wise; he could see everything which he had not seen before, understand everything and know everything, both what is good and what is bad. Adam and Eve were allowed to eat to their hearts' content from all the other trees in Paradise Garden; only from the tree of the knowledge of good and evil did the dear Lord forbid them to eat.

Among the other animals in Paradise there lived

also the snake. But you must not think that the snake in Paradise had the same form that she has today and crept upon her belly. O no! At that time she was a beautiful animal with graceful little feet, a long striped neck, and a wonderful skin which changed as she moved to all the colors of the rainbow. The snake looked upon all the other animals with pride and scorn; she considered herself wiser than any one in the whole world, and everybody else on the contrary very silly and foolish; she felt she could get the better of all of them put together. But she was really no shrewder than the other animals, she was only falser and more deceitful. Her heart was jealous and wicked, and she could not bear the sight of Adam because he had not chosen her for his wife. She hated Eve with her whole heart. But she acted the hypocrite, was friendly to her and spoke fine words, because she was false, as false as only snakes can be.

It happened one day that the snake and Eve met by chance at the tree of knowledge.

"Didn't God tell you that you might eat of all the trees in Paradise Garden?" she began slyly. But Eve answered:

"God has allowed us to eat of all the trees in Paradise, except the tree of the knowledge of good and evil."

Then the snake smiled and said:

"If you eat of the tree of knowledge, you will become wise like God himself, and you can create worlds as He himself did. God just doesn't want you to become as wise as He. But you certainly won't die of it."

Then she began to act as if she wished to play with

Eve and pushed her lightly against the tree, till Eve touched the fruit. Eve was terribly frightened at this and cried out:

"What are you doing?"

But the snake said:

"See, you have touched the fruit of the tree of knowledge and it didn't kill you. God only wanted to make you afraid."

The snake spoke such words in order to tempt Eve; she plucked a fine tasty apple from the tree of knowledge and held it out for Eve to eat. Eve was a very inquisitive woman and wished very much to know what kind of a queer apple it was. So she allowed herself to be persuaded by the sly, deceitful snake and ate of the fruit. Scarcely, however, had she taken a bite when she began to feel very afraid and anxious, and she thought that she would have to die all alone. So she went to Adam and persuaded him to eat of the apple also, and Adam ate of the forbidden fruit.

Immediately after that they both became very wise, and could understand and know everything. For the first time they knew that they were naked and they were ashamed before each other; so they made themselves clothes out of fig leaves and put them on.

Then a sharp wind blew suddenly through Paradise Garden and Adam and Eve recognized therein the voice of God.

"Adam, Adam, what have you done? Have you not eaten of the tree of which I forbade you to eat?"

In his fear Adam did not know anything to answer, so he said:

"Eve gave me the apple."

Then the Lord said:

"Eve, Eve, what have you done?"

"The crafty snake tempted me."

Then the Lord's wrath was kindled, and He said to Adam:

"From now on you must work hard, and in the sweat of your brow shall you earn your bread."

And God cursed Adam and Eve and everything that belonged to them: the earth, so that it no longer gave bread and rolls ready-made; the wine, so that it was no longer served in cups of red rose-leaves; the flowers, so that they faded and vanished away; He cursed everything else that was around them. And God drove Adam and Eve out of Paradise; He sent two fiery angels down to earth who stood with naked swords before the gate of Paradise so that Adam and Eve could not enter again.

From that time on, Adam and Eve led a hard and troubled life. Adam had to work from early morning till late at night. He dug and shovelled, he sowed the seed, ground the grain, kneaded the loaf and baked the bread. Thorns and thistles grew up out of the earth, which were no good to any one; they made the work harder for Adam and pricked his hands and feet. And God also punished the snake that had led Eve into such temptation; so she lost her lovely graceful little feet and from that time on had to creep upon her belly. She had to atone for her pride and become ugly, so ugly that men feel a loathing for her. And since that time there has been hatred between mankind and the snake, even to the present day.

CAIN AND ABEL

When Adam and Eve were driven out of Paradise Garden they began to work. Adam tilled the soil and Eve took care of the house. They lived together in peace and were very fond of each other. And the Lord sent them two sons: Cain and Abel.

When these two had grown up, they were talking together one day and Abel said to Cain:

"Let us divide the world between us."

Cain consented to that and they agreed that all the soil should belong to Cain and all the sheep to Abel. Thus Cain became a farmer and Abel a shepherd.

So it happened, some time afterwards, that Abel brought a present to God of his loveliest little sheep, and Cain gave the fruit of the earth. God was very much pleased with Abel's gift and accepted it graciously; but he did not wish to take Cain's present, we do not know why... but I think it was because Cain did not give it willingly.

Then Cain grew jealous of his brother Abel and soon began to quarrel with him. He would no longer allow Abel's sheep to graze upon his fields, and he said:

"The earth is mine."

Abel on the other hand did not wish to give his brother any of his sheep's wool for clothing, and he said:

"The sheep belong to me."

Then Cain became furious, and shouted out to him:

"Pasture your sheep in the air, if you can."

But Abel answered:

"Ask the earth to give you wool for clothing."

And thus the quarrelsome talk flew back and forth from early morning till late at night, and the wrangling never came to an end.

Then one day it happened that Cain fell into a wild rage in the midst of this; he seized his axe which was near at hand and struck at his brother till Abel sank down to the earth, dead. Until that time men had not known what death is, hence Cain did not understand what was wrong with his brother and believed that Abel had fallen into a deep sleep. He tried to waken him, but Abel did not stir. So Cain let him lie still. When night came on, Cain wanted to go home and called to his brother:

"Stand up, brother, it is now dark, and time for us to go home."

But Abel lay there—he did not move, and gave no answer. Then Cain lifted him up, shook him and cried:

"Brother Abel, do stand up!"

All his pains, however, were in vain. Then Cain saw that something dreadful had happened to his brother, but he did not know what it was. And all at once he felt a pain in his heart, and clear, hot drops ran from his eyes. He took one of the drops in his hand, looked at it carefully from every side, but did not know what it was. Meanwhile the sly fox came walking along. So Cain said to him:

"Good fox, you have been round the world, even before my father Adam came—please tell me, what has happened to my brother, and what is the meaning of these clear little drops that have run from my eyes for the first time today?"

And the fox, who was so very wise that he knew how to explain everything at once, said:

"Your brother is dead; for since your Mother Eve ate of the tree of knowledge, men must die, whether they want to or not. The clear tiny drops, as bright and shining and transparent as precious jewels, are tears. For with death, tears also came into the world."

When Cain comprehended the meaning of these wise words, he was terribly alarmed over what he had done, and because he was very afraid of the Lord he crept into a cave. But he had been there only a little while when he heard the stern voice of God:

"Cain, where is your brother?"

And Cain said:

"I do not know; am I my brother's keeper?"

Then God said:

"Why do you hide yourself from me? You have killed your brother, and his blood cries unto me from the ground!"

And God cursed Cain and said:

"Cursed shall you be upon the earth which has received your brother's blood. A fugitive and a wanderer shall you be upon the earth and nowhere shall you find rest. The soil which you till shall give you no harvest."

Then for the first time Cain realized his crime; he begged the Lord for mercy and said:

"You drive me from the land and I must hide myself; lonely and accursed, I must wander about the world, and any one who finds me can put me to death."

Then God had compassion upon Cain and made a mark on his forehead so that no one should slay him.

And from that time on, it was a sorrowful life that Cain led, full of grief, distress and torment. He arose and went, and wandered day and night over hills and valleys, and nowhere could he find rest. The earth trembled beneath his feet, the sun grew dark above his head, the moon hid herself in the clouds and left him behind in the darkness; the wind whipped and drove him from place to place, the flowers withered along his way as soon as he came near them, the little birds were silenced in their lovely song, the trees stopped their rustling and gave the tired wanderer no shade. The animals ran away from him and men fled when they saw the mark upon his forehead. Never was there a sadder journey than this, never a man who atoned more heavily for his sin than Cain.

Cain felt deep remorse. He searched his heart, acknowledged his sin, and did severe penance many long years; so God finally had pity on him and took the dreadful curse away. Cain thanked the Lord humbly for His mercy, and commenced a new life. Soon he was no longer lonely, for he wooed a lovely young woman and married her. And because they loved each other, God sent them a son and they named him Enoch. They lived many, many years, and Cain was very industrious, clever and godly; he built a whole city and called it Enoch after his son.

NOAH AND HIS ARK

There were many, many people on the earth, but they were bad at heart, corrupt, tricky and violent. So God wanted to destroy them from the face of the earth. Among all the wicked people, however, there was one man named Noah who was pious and good, and God wished to let Noah live. So He called him to Him and said:

"I will destroy every living thing upon the earth and I will cause a great flood of many waters to come. Everything that lives upon the earth shall perish. But with you I will enter into a covenant, because you are pious and good. Build for yourself a great ark out of fir-trees and take up your dwelling within it, you and your wife, your sons and your sons' wives and all kinds of animals. When the deluge comes all the other creatures will perish, but your ark will float upon the water and you only will be saved, you and all your house."

When Noah heard these words, he was glad at

heart; he went home and planted a very great many fir-trees. But when the people saw this, they laughed at Noah and made fun of him and said:

"What are you doing that for?"

But Noah did not trouble himself over their talk and their ridicule. He thought to himself: "Laugh all you wish; I know what I know."

When the seeds which Noah had planted in the earth had grown up into big trees, he went out and cut them down, and began to build an ark, three hundred cubits long, fifty cubits wide and thirty cubits high. On one side of the ark he made a door and at the top a very little window. He filled up the crevices inside and out with pitch, so that no water could get in. And in the middle of the ark Noah placed a precious jewel, large and very beautiful from which came glittering rays that lighted up the whole place.

Then the people laughed again at Noah and his work, and they jeered at him. But this time also Noah did not bother about their talk and their ridicule and thought to himself: "Just laugh all you please; I know what I know."

When Noah had at last finished his ark, God said to him:

"Go into the ark, you and your whole household, and take into the ark with you from all living creatures, two of every kind—one pair, male and female. I will save them together with you, so that after the flood they may multiply and grow and fill the earth."

Then Noah said to God:

"But where shall I get them all? There are crea-

tures that live far, far away from here, on distant islands
where no man has ever set his foot, and birds that soar
high in the air, animals that stay in the dark depths of
the forests, and fish hidden deep in the sea, worms
squeezed in the heart of stones,—tell me, dear Lord,
where shall I get them all?"

And God answered:

"I will send them to you."

On a beautiful morning, as Noah was sitting at the
door of his ark, and the sun was shining brightly over
the earth, they all arrived, a pair of every kind, male
and female. They bowed respectfully before Noah and
said:

"Noah, we have come to ask you to take us into
your ark with you, because we have learned that a great
flood is to come upon the earth."

Then Noah did as God had told him; he led them
into the ark and assigned a place to each one.

When they were all in the ark, the windows of
heaven were opened and rain fell upon the earth; it
rained forty long days and forty nights without stop-
ping. The waters rose and swirled till the highest peaks
of the mountains were covered. Then everything that
lived upon the earth was destroyed. And round about
there was nothing to be seen except water and sky. But
upon the water floated the ark with Noah, his family,
and all the living creatures that God wished to save.

In those days, Noah had a great deal to do, for he
had to feed the animals and provide them with everything which they needed. This he did to please God, in

order to preserve the lives of all the creatures that God wished to save.

Noah had his troubles keeping everything in the ark in order, for soon there was squabbling and disputing everywhere. If the animals did not get their food at the right time, they growled and scolded and made a great noise; they talked a lot of scandal, too, and lied and spoke evil of one another. Noah cursed, scolded and struck blows at them. When all this did not help, Noah threatened to throw the disobedient ones into the water. Then the animals were scared, and from that time on peace reigned in the ark.

When the forty days were over, God remembered Noah and his ark; He shut the windows of heaven, and sent a wind down to earth to dry everything. The wind had scarcely arrived when the rain stopped and the waters fell. But only after a hundred and fifty days did the peaks of the mountains appear, and Noah's ark came to rest upon Mount Ararat. Then Noah opened the tiny window and sent out a raven to see how far the waters had fallen. The raven flew here and there, and came back into the ark. Noah waited another seven days, and then he opened the little window again and let a dove fly out. But the dove could not find a dry place to rest anywhere, so it flew back and perched on the roof of the ark. Noah reached his hand out and brought the dove inside. After that Noah waited once more for seven days and again sent out the dove. At evening it came back, and in its beak there was an olive leaf. This was a good sign, and then Noah knew that the waters had fallen.

THE TOWER OF BABEL

When God had allowed the flood to pass and when the waters had dried up from the earth, Noah opened the door of his ark and let all the living creatures that had been saved along with him, go wherever they pleased. They scattered over the whole earth. The people had children, increased in number and soon the big world was again inhabited.

But they were always afraid that God might send down another flood upon them, so they came together to consider among themselves what they could do about it. And some of them said:

"Do you know what we'll do? We'll build a tower so high that its top will reach to heaven. Then if God sends punishment upon us, we can climb from it into heaven and beg Him for mercy."

Such words pleased every one very much, and soon the people began to build the tower. However, as they had neither stones nor lime, they used bricks and pitch instead.

They were very industrious and worked constantly, and the tower rose higher and higher. But the Lord was not pleased that people wanted to climb so high; He grew exceedingly angry over this vain idea and determined to punish their pride. So one night He came down to earth and confused their speech. The next morning when the men began to work, each one spoke a different language, and they could not make one another understand anything at all. From that time on things went very strangely: if one of them called another to pass him the bricks, he brought him pitch; if he asked for pitch, he received bricks.... And so it went on and on continually, and no matter what they did, nobody understood what the others said. Everything went upside down, whatever they did was always wrong.

Soon discord arose among them, and they quarrelled and struck one another. They no longer worked at the tower but let it stand unfinished. Since that time all men speak different languages and no one understands the words of another until he has mastered them by hard study and diligence.

OUR FATHER ABRAHAM

It came to pass in those days that men did not
know the real God, and believed in many, many gods,
and in idols which they themselves made out of stone
and wood; they served these gods and brought gifts to
them. A man was living then, named Terah, who dealt
in idols. The rich and the poor came to him when they
wanted any, and bought according to their means—the
rich buying big idols and the poor, small ones. One fine
day a little son was born to the idol-merchant and he
was named Abraham. The child grew to be a very wise
boy; he was always serious and thoughtful and soon
formed his own opinions about everything. He saw how
people prayed to the idols which his father made, and
this did not seem right to him. He thought to himself
that the true God could not be made by men's hands—
He must be mightier and more powerful than men, and
He must be everywhere by day and by night. Thus

thought little Abraham, and he never stopped seeking for the dear Lord.

At first, when he saw the sun rise over the world, shining so brilliantly, he thought for a while that the sun was the real God, and he was very glad. But the sun sank and disappeared, and then little Abraham knew that it could not be God. When night came and the moon glittered over the world in her silvery glory, and the golden stars sparkled so gaily down from above, he believed again for awhile that they were real gods. But the moon also faded with approaching day and the stars grew dim. Then Abraham knew again that these were not real gods; he grew very sad and cried bitterly. However, he was soon comforted with the thought: "God must be still higher than sun, moon and stars and must be ruler over the whole big world."

It happened one day that his father gave him a basket full of idols and sent him with it to the market-place. The rich and the poor came there and wanted to buy the idols from him. They asked little Abraham if his idols performed miracles, and Abraham answered:

"Yes, they perform miracles, but only after you have paid the price."

Then the people paid the price for the idols, and took them away. Little Abraham, however, when he had the money in his pocket, laughed aloud, made fun of the purchasers and said:

"How can you expect these gods to do wonders, gods which my father made with his own hands out of wood and stone?"

Then the people grew very angry, demanded their

money back and threw the idols into Abraham's basket.

And Abraham got all his wares together and took them back to his father.

Old Terah then saw that his son was no merchant, and he set him to watch over the idols. But while Abraham kept watch, people came and brought gifts and sacrifices. One day an old woman reached out a bowl full of dainty food to the gods. Little Abraham waited a minute till he was all alone, then set the plate out of the way, took a stick and smashed the idols to pieces. He spared only one very big idol and put the stick in its hand, but the nice morsels of food he ate up himself. Shortly afterward his father came, and when he saw the broken idols, he was beside himself with rage and screamed at his son:

"You good-for-nothing, what kind of a mess have you made?"

"I didn't do it," replied Abraham. "An old woman brought things for the gods to eat, and they all threw themselves greedily at the bowl. So the big god got mad, he took the stick and beat the others till they were all smashed. Then he grabbed the bowl and ate everything up." The father knew very well that Abraham had done all this himself, and notified the king. Abraham was summoned to appear before the king and had to explain why he had broken up the idols.

Then Abraham answered the king:

"I destroyed the idols because I do not believe in them. I believe only in the one, true and all-powerful God!"

At this the king was enraged and pronounced a

terrible judgment upon Abraham; he must be thrown into a fiery furnace and be burned up alive. This was done. But Abraham was untouched by the flames. Then the king and all the people assembled around him saw that a miracle had happened. They recognized that the God of Abraham was the true and only God.

נ֗־־

HOW ABRAHAM CAME TO
KNOW GOD

Abraham arose and went out into the wide world to search for God. He wandered many, many years and was getting to be an old man, yet he had never found God. Once when he had grown very tired on his wanderings, he lay down in a field, hoping to rest a little. He had lain in the grass only a short time when he heard a heap of little worms talking together: "Just look at that man, he's going around the world hunting everywhere for God and doesn't know where He is; but we know."

When Abraham heard these words, he laughed and said:

"You're certainly a conceited little people. Men know nothing as yet about God, and you think you know everything!"

But the little worms let him talk and did not trouble themselves about him, because they knew what they knew. And Abraham continued on his way and meditated upon the thought of how long he still must wander until he found God.

Then all at once there was a whirring in the air—a flock of birds flew by and sang a song in their flight praising God and His goodness.

And Abraham laughed again at the innocence of the birds and said:

"You, too, are a conceited little people. Men know nothing at all about God and you think you know everything!"

But the little birds let him talk; they did not trouble themselves about him and flew away, because they knew what they knew. Abraham, however, went his way. He had not gone very far, when he met a herd of animals. It was early morning. With uplifted heads, they lay stretched out in the forest and sent forth a song. Then Abraham spoke to them and said: "What are you singing?"

"We are singing a song of praise to God," the animals answered him, "and every living creature does this every morning when it wakes from sleep—each in its own way."

And Abraham asked again:

"How do you really know that there is a God?"

The animals were astonished at such words and they said:

"Who would take care of us if there were no God? He alone sees even the tiniest creature, thinks of it and sends it its daily bread; nothing is hidden from His eyes. A very small worm among our kinsfolk, living in the dark depths of the rocks—God cares for it, too, and sends it food. You need only to split open the rock and you will see that what we say is the truth."

Abraham broke a crevice in the rock and saw the little worm creeping inside. And he asked it:

"Where do you get anything to eat? Who knows that you live hidden in there?"

Thereupon the little worm answered:

"The Lord in heaven is the Father of all creatures; He knows also that I live here and He provides me with food."

Then Abraham saw that the animals spoke the truth and rejoiced that he at last had found God.

GOD REVEALS HIMSELF TO
ABRAHAM

When Abraham had learned from the animals who
the true God is, his heart grew warm and happy, and
he prayed to God and asked if He would not show Himself to him. In the night he stretched out his arms to
heaven above and begged for a sign, saying:

"God, give me a sign of Your presence, for I want
to serve You with my whole heart."

And God heard Abraham's prayer and sent a great
weariness over his limbs, so that he sank to the earth
and was wrapped in a deep sleep. Then God appeared
to Abraham in a dream, and talked with him, saying:

"I am God, whom you seek, the great and all-
powerful One from whom nothing is hidden. I remember the very smallest creature and provide it with food.
The grass growing in the meadows, the flower giving
out its perfume in the garden, the little bird flying in
the heavens, the fish swimming in the water—all is

according to My will. But with you I will make a covenant for all eternity, with you and with your children after you, because you did not want to believe in the gods made of wood and have sought after Me. I will bless them that bless you, and curse them that curse you, and in you shall all the families of the earth be blest. And I will give to you and to your children the whole land of Canaan for an everlasting dwelling-place, and I will make you the father of many people."

When Abraham awoke he prayed to God and thanked Him for appearing to him in a dream. He said:

"O God, my Lord, I have seen You in a dream and I have recognized You; but I do not know how to explain Your words; their meaning is dark and hidden from me. What do You wish to give me? I have no children at all, and one of my household shall be my heir. But You say that You will give the land of Canaan to me and to my children. How shall I interpret Your words?"

Then God appeared a second time and said:

"Abraham, look up toward the heavens and count the stars. Are you able to number them? You shall have even that many children; they shall be a separate people and they shall be called Jews. But the land of Israel shall be their native land."

Then Abraham believed the word of God and he built a temple on the spot where the Lord had appeared unto him.

THE ANGELS APPEAR TO
ABRAHAM

Abraham and Sarah his wife were already old and had lived many long years together. But they had no children. They were very unhappy over this and thought that they never would have any. But the dear Lord wished to comfort them in their sorrow; He gave a son to their maid-servant Hagar and presented him to Abraham. And Abraham took him and named him Ishmael. But Ishmael was a wild, ill-mannered boy and gave his father nothing but trouble. Abraham grieved a great deal over this; he prayed to God and begged Him to let Sarah have a son. And God heard Abraham's prayer.

It was on a beautiful summer day, as Abraham was sitting at the door of his tent that three men came walking along, and when Abraham saw them, he ran toward them, bowed low before them and said:

"I beg of you, do not pass by my house, but stop with me. We will bring water to wash your feet. Sit down under the tree and I will get you some bread.

When you have rested, and have had something to eat and drink, then you may go on."

The men were satisfied with this and stayed with Abraham.

Abraham was a very hospitable man and no stranger was allowed to pass his house without having rested and eaten there. So he ran inside to Sarah and said:

"Hurry up, Sarah, mix three measures of flour, knead it into dough and bake a cake." Then he went on to the cattle, took a tender young calf and gave it to a servant who quickly prepared it for eating. And Abraham served butter and milk, with meat from the calf which had been dressed. He set everything before them and then stood beside them under the tree, while they ate.

When the men had eaten and rested, they rose thanked Abraham for his hospitality and said:

"In a year we will come back; then Sarah your wife shall have a son."

But Sarah, who was standing behind the door of the tent and heard these words, laughed at the idea that she should have a son when she was no longer young.

Then the men asked Abraham:

"Why does Sarah laugh? Is anything impossible with God? In the next year, at this time, we will come to you again and Sarah shall have a son."

And it happened as they said: after a year had passed Sarah bore a son and they named him Isaac.

The men, however, whom Abraham had entertained in his tent had not been mortals; they were angels whom God had sent to Abraham with the glad news.

SODOM AND GOMORRAH

When the angels had delivered their message to Abraham, they turned their steps toward the city of Sodom, for through them God wished to destroy that city, because it was sinful and very wicked.

The people who lived in Sodom were spiteful, tricky and evil, and the holy law of hospitality was never once observed by them. If it happened that a stranger stopped at Sodom and asked shelter for the night, he was well received. But if the bed in which he was to spend the night was too long for him, his legs were pulled out until his feet reached to the end of the bed. If the bed was too short, the guest's feet were simply chopped off.—Once a little girl out of pity had given a poor man a piece of bread. The wicked people heard of this, seized the child, stuck her in a vat, filled it with honey and set it on the roof. Then the bees came from every direction and ate her up together with the honey.—Such terrible things and even much worse ones happened there daily, and therefore the people of Sodom were to be destroyed.

God considered, however, whether He should tell Abraham anything about His plans or not; He said to Himself:

"How can I hide from Abraham what I intend to do, when I have entered into a covenant with him?" So finally He told him. Then Abraham prayed to God and said:

"Will You destroy the righteous with the wicked? Maybe there will be fifty righteous people in the city; will You destroy all of them? That is far from being like You, when You are the Judge of all the earth! You will not pass such judgment!"

And God said to Abraham:

"If I find fifty righteous in the city, I will spare the whole place for their sakes."

But Abraham talked further with God and begged Him humbly:

"Maybe only forty-five righteous people live in Sodom; will You then destroy them all?"

And God said:

"If I find only forty-five good people in the city, I will not destroy them."

Then Abraham said:

"Do not be angry with me, Lord, for talking still more, but there may probably be only thirty good people in Sodom, maybe only twenty...."

And God answered:

"I will not destroy the city even if there are only twenty."

Then Abraham plucked up all his courage and said:

"O, do not be angry, Lord, that I beg once more, but maybe only ten righteous will be found in Sodom. Will You then also save the city?"

And God answered:

"I will forgive it for the sake of even ten."

But when He had searched with care, He found not a single righteous person among all the people of Sodom, so they had to perish.

It was toward evening when the angels arrived at Sodom. Lot, the son of Abraham's brother, sat at the gate of the city and when he saw them, he arose, went towards them, bowed low and said:

"My good lords, stop with me and remain overnight; let your feet be washed and tomorrow, when you have rested, go your way."

But the angels said:

"We wish to abide in the street all night."

Lot begged them so heartily to stay with him and accept his hospitality that they granted his wish. Then he prepared a meal for them and baked unleavened bread which they ate. But before they could lie down to rest, the people of Sodom came, surrounded Lot's house, made a terrible noise and cried out:

"Who are the men who have come to see you? Bring them out!"

Then Lot went out to them before the house, shut the door behind him and said to them:

"I beg of you, brethren, do nothing evil to these good men. If you wish, I will give you my own children, but I will not deliver these men unto you, because they are my guests and are staying under the shelter of my roof!"

When the men of Sodom realized the meaning of these words, they grew furious, rushed upon him, pushed him aside forcefully and cried out:

"Stand back! You want to teach us how we should treat strangers! You're the only stranger among us and you want to rule!"

So they talked; they rushed at the door and wanted to break it open. The angels, however, who were inside Lot's house, struck the wicked men with blindness, so that they could no longer find the door. They ran here and there, fell over one another, fought and raged till they were tired out. Then the angels said to Lot:

"If you have any sons and daughters in this city, get them all together and leave this place, for God has sent us to destroy Sodom."

Lot hesitated; then the angels seized him and his wife and children by the hand, and as the red dawn arose they left the city. And the angels said to them:

"If you wish to escape with your life, do not look back to the city!"

But Lot's wife was very inquisitive and she thought to herself that nobody would notice it, if she looked back just a little bit. She did so, and in an instant she was turned into a pillar of salt.

And God rained down fire and brimstone from heaven upon Sodom and Gomorrah and He destroyed those cities.

ISHMAEL

After Isaac had been born to Sarah, she was afraid that he might learn many bad things from the wild Ishmael, so she spoke to her husband and begged him to drive Ishmael and Hagar his mother out of the house. But Abraham was a good man; he had pity upon the two and did not want to do this. But Sarah gave him no peace and bothered him so long that he finally did what she asked. One fine day Abraham rose early, took a piece of bread, and a bottle of water, and put it on Hagar's shoulder; he gave her the boy and told her to leave his house. Then Hagar took her child in her arms and went off into the wilderness.

Soon, however, the bread was finished and the bottle of water empty, the child wanted a drink, and cried and moaned with thirst. And Hagar wandered around in the wilderness day and night and could not find a spring anywhere. Then she laid her child under a bush, and went a long way off from him, because she could not bear to see him die.

But God heard the wailing of little Ishmael and the angel of the Lord called down from Heaven to Hagar:

"What is the matter with you, Hagar? Do not be afraid. Rise up, take your boy and lead him by the hand. He will grow to be a man, he will have children, and God will make him the father of a great nation because he is the son of Abraham."

When Hagar heard these words she was happy in her heart and thanked God for His goodness. And as she went toward her child, all at once she saw a spring very near her. She went to it, filled her bottle with water and gave Ishmael a drink. And Ishmael was revived, so that he was soon able to wander farther along with his mother.

Hagar and Ishmael lived for many years in the wilderness. Ishmael grew, and became a strong, brave man and a fine archer. After a while he married a woman out of the land of Egypt. They had many children, these in turn had many children, and so they became a great people.

ABRAHAM AND ISHMAEL

After many long years, Abraham remembered his
son Ishmael, and wanted to see him. So he arose, saddled his ass and went off into the wilderness to Ishmael's
house. But when he took leave of his wife Sarah, she
implored him not to get down from his ass; she begged
him just to ride to the house and then turn back at once,
because she was afraid he might stay much longer. He
promised this to her and went his way.—It was about
noonday when Abraham arrived at his son's house, and
Ishmael's wife stood on the threshold. Then he spoke
to her and said:

"Where is Ishmael?"

And she answered him:

"He has gone with his mother to get some fruit."

Then he asked her kindly:

"Please give me a piece of bread and a drink of
water."

But the wife answered:

"We have no bread and no water."

So Abraham took leave of her and told her to say to her husband that an old man from the land of Canaan had been there and had left word that the door of the house was not hospitable. When Ishmael returned home that night, his wife told him about the strange old man and repeated his words. Ishmael knew very well that the stranger was his father, and understood the meaning of his words, for Abraham meant nothing else but that the wife was a wicked woman. So Ishmael drove her out of his house and took another woman for his wife.

Some time had passed, and Abraham again wanted to see Ishmael. Again he made ready, saddled his ass and rode off into the wilderness. When he left his wife Sarah, she again implored him not to get off his ass, and begged him just to ride to the house and turn back again, for she was afraid he might stay a much longer time with his son. He promised her this and went his way.

And again it was about noon when Abraham stopped before Ishmael's house. On the threshold stood Ishmael's second wife. He addressed her and said:

"Where is Ishmael?"

And she answered:

"Ishmael has gone with Hagar to feed the asses."

Then Abraham asked her kindly:

"Will you give me a piece of bread and a drink of water?"

And the wife ran into the house and brought him something to eat and drink.

Abraham thanked her and asked her to tell her

husband that an old man from the land of Canaan had been there and had left word that his threshold was hospitable and that he wished him and his house happiness and prosperity.

When Ishmael returned from his work, his wife told him about the old man and repeated his message. But Ishmael knew very well that the old man was his father and also grasped the meaning of his words, for Abraham this time had praised his wife. And Ishmael embraced his wife and was deeply pleased with her.

THE SACRIFICING OF ISAAC

Abraham became a rich man. He had many lambs, sheep and cattle, and much land; he had gold in plenty, and was king in the land where he lived. His son Isaac was growing to be a strong and wise boy. Sarah loved Isaac tenderly, and indulged her only son as much as she possibly could.

On the day when Isaac was to be weaned from his mother, Abraham arranged a great feast and invited guests from far and near. The food was served in golden bowls, eaten from golden plates, and the guests drank from golden goblets. They ate and drank, praised the fine-looking and wise young boy, and extolled the hospitality of the host.

But Satan wanted to ruin the pious Abraham. So he went to the Lord and said:

"Great Heavens! Just look at the way Your favorite Abraham is honoring his son. He has invited the whole world to the feast, but to You who gave him this son he hasn't offered even a dove."

Then God said to Satan:

"Abraham has given this feast in honor of his son; but if I ask of him this only son himself as a sacrifice, he will give him to me."

But Satan laughed a wicked and doubting laugh and said:

"I'd have to see that!"

So one day God appeared to Abraham in the field where he was digging a well and said:

"You will have to bring me your son Isaac for a burnt-offering."

Then Abraham said:

"Very well, I will do it."

And he did not show the least bit how much it pained him.

The next morning Abraham arose at daybreak, saddled his ass, took wood and fire for the burnt-offering and made himself ready for the journey. Then he went into the bedroom where Isaac was sleeping beside his mother and wakened him. Sarah was very much surprised because, until then, Isaac had always remained at her side, and she asked Abraham:

"Where are you going with the boy?"

Abraham pretended that he had nothing special in his mind, and said:

"Well, of course, dear wife, you have spoiled him a lot; the boy is growing big and must learn something worth while."

Then Sarah realized that her husband was right,

put on the boy's clothes, and got him ready for the
journey. But at parting she fondled and kissed him
to the very end, and only with a heavy heart did she
let him go.

So Abraham set off with Isaac and two men-
servants, and they went toward the land of Moriah,
where Isaac was to be sacrified. After they had been
travelling along for a little while, Satan came toward
them in the form of an old man and addressed Abraham:

"Abraham, what are you planning to do?"

"I am on my way to offer prayers to God," answered Abraham.

"But why are you taking the axe and wood along?"

"It may be that we shall stop longer on the way
and that we shall need them to cook our food."

Then Satan held back no longer and said:

"You old fool, do you think I don't know where
you're going and what you're intending to do? Have you
waited for your son a hundred years, and now are you
going to sacrifice him like an animal?"

Thus spoke Satan. For he wanted to stir up Abraham against the command of God. But Abraham only
looked up to heaven and said humbly:

"It is God's will."

Then Satan saw that he could not accomplish anything that way, so he changed himself quickly into a
pond and obstructed Abraham's way. Abraham however
would not allow himself to be led aside; with Isaac and
his servants he waded deeper and deeper into the water,
till it soon reached up to their necks. In his distress
Abraham cried out to God for help and scarcely had he

done so when the water was dried up.—On the third day when Abraham saw the place afar off which God had indicated to him, he said to his servants:

"Stay here with the ass, I will go up into the mountain with Isaac, and when we have prayed, we will come again to you."

And Abraham took the wood for the burnt-offering, laid it on his son Isaac's shoulders, took the knife in his hand and together they went up into the mountain.

On the way Isaac asked his father:

"We have fire and wood, Father, what are we going to do with them?"

"We will offer sacrifice to God," said Abraham.

"And where is the sheep for the burnt-offering?" asked the boy again.

"The little sheep, the little sheep...we'll find it soon," answered Abraham, because he didn't know what he should say to his son. But when they reached the mountain-top, he said to Isaac:

"The lamb, my son, which we are to offer up to God is you yourself. Will you make this sacrifice to Him?"

Isaac was a devout child and said simply: "Yes."

Then he begged his father to bind his hands and feet so that he could not resist. Abraham did this; he bound Isaac fast, and laid him on the altar on top of the wood, took the knife and was about to sacrifice him. But in that instant, he heard the voice of an angel who called to him:

"Abraham, Abraham, do not lay hands on your son,

and do no harm to him, because now I know that you fear the Lord and are submissive to him."

When Abraham heard these words he was glad at heart. And as he looked around he saw a ram in the bushes; it was caught by its horns in a thicket, and could not get out. Then Abraham took the animal and laid it on the altar-stone in Isaac's stead. But when Isaac saw the ram bound upon the altar, he ran up to it, kissed it on the head and said:

"Little sheep, little sheep, may your blood which will be shed for me be just as dear to the Lord as my blood, and your body as my body." And they sacrificed the ram to God.

Then again Abraham heard a voice, and the angel of God spoke to him once more from heaven:

"Abraham! Because you have been willing to sacrifice what is dearest to you, I will bless you and your children."

Abraham thanked God for His mercy, took Isaac and hurried home with him, to share the glad news with Sarah.

But Satan, who had had no luck with Abraham and who now wished to revenge himself upon him, ran to Abraham's house, hid himself under the window and pondered upon what evil thing he could do to him. Sarah sat in the room and waited with longing heart for Isaac's return. When he did not come for such a long time, she grew restless and troubled and felt great anxiety. All at once she heard close under her window the moaning voice of her child:

"Mother, Mother, Father has hurt me."

It was however Satan who was imitating Isaac's voice.

Then Sarah was terribly frightened and ran to the window to look after her child. But nobody was at the window and nobody came into the room. Yet the same voice wailed on:

"Mother, dear Mother, Father has killed me and thrown my body to the birds on the roof."

When Sarah heard these words she was seized with a horror of what had happened, her heart shrank together convulsively, and she sank down to the earth, dead. So when Isaac came home, he had no mother.

ELIEZER AND REBEKAH

When Isaac had grown up, Abraham thought about getting a wife for him. He called the oldest servant of his household to him, talked with him and said:

"I am an old man and can no longer go out into the world to seek a wife for my son. Go to Mesopotamia, look among the daughters of the land for the most beautiful and best, and bring her as a wife for my son."

Eliezer promised his master that he would grant his wish. He took ten camels and loaded them with very precious things; then he arose and started for Mesopotamia. Toward evening he arrived at the city of Nahor. It was about the time when the women went to draw water from the well. He stopped his camels at the well and said to himself:

"I will lie here and wait, and when a maiden comes to whom I shall say, 'Let down your pitcher and let me drink from it,' and she will give me and my camels to drink, then she is the wife whom God has appointed for Isaac."

Scarcely had he said this, when a young girl came down to the well; she was slender and beautiful, and carried a pitcher upon her shoulder. She drew water from the well, and started away. Then Eliezer ran after her, spoke to her and said:

"Maiden, let me drink a little water out of your pitcher."

And she answered him: "Drink, my lord,"—letting down her pitcher and giving him to drink.

When he had refreshed himself with the water to his heart's content, she hurried to the camels and gave them also to drink. Then Eliezer knew that God had chosen this girl to be the wife of his lord's son. He took a golden ring and two magnificent bracelets and gave them to her saying:

"Whose daughter are you, my child? Is there room in your father's house for me to lodge overnight?"

And the girl answered:

"I am Rebekah, the daughter of Bethuel. There is plenty of room in my father's house to give you lodging, and also straw and fodder for the camels."

When Eliezer heard these words, he thanked God for his goodness and accompanied by Rebekah went to her home. But Rebekah hurried on ahead, told her family of her meeting with the stranger and showed them the ring and the bracelets. When Rebekah's brother Laban heard this and saw the costly presents, he went to meet the man and invited him to stop at his father's house. He gave him water to wash his feet, and offered him food and drink. He ungirded the camels and gave them straw and fodder.

Eliezer however pushed aside the food and drink, because he wished first to give his message; and he said:

"I am Eliezer, the servant of Abraham. God has blest my master, and has given him sheep and oxen, camels and asses, silver and gold, maid-servants and men-servants. His wife Sarah has borne him an only son. A short time ago my master called me to him, and commanded me to go into the land of his fathers, and from among his kindred there to choose a wife for Isaac. Then I set out on my way to fulfill his command. At evening I came to the city of Nahor, stopped to rest at the well with my camels, waited for the maidens who come to the well and said to myself: If a maiden comes to the well, to whom I shall say, 'Let down your pitcher and give me to drink from it,' and she will give me and my camels to drink, she will be the wife whom God has provided for Isaac. Then came Rebekah to the well, and gave me and my camels to drink.—If you will deal well by my master, then tell me so; otherwise I will arise and go my way."

Then spoke Rebekah's father and her brother:

"We will give her to you very willingly. But it is the custom with us that the maiden too must be asked her wishes. If she wants to become the wife of your young master, then take her with you unto Isaac, for it is God's will."

They called Rebekah and asked her, and Rebekah declared herself willing to go with Eliezer to the land of Canaan. Eliezer was very happy over this, and gave Rebekah wonderful presents: fine clothing, gold and silver ornaments and rare jewels. He gave gifts to her

mother and brother also. Then finally they sat down
to the table and ate and drank.

Rebekah stayed a few days longer in her parents'
home, was very happy over all her precious and lovely
gifts and then said good-bye to her women-friends. Her
father and mother were anxious to keep her longer, but
Eliezer was in a hurry to take her to his master's house.
So Rebekah made herself ready with her handmaidens,
and went with Eliezer into the land where Abraham
dwelt.

It happened that about the time when Eliezer arrived with Rebekah before the city, Isaac had gone into
the fields, and so they met each other. Rebekah hur-
riedly got down from her camel and asked Eliezer:

"Who is the man coming to meet us?"

And Eliezer answered:

"That is Isaac, your bridegroom."

Then Rebekah grew very embarrassed and covered
her face with her veil. But Isaac came directly to her,
took her by the hand and led her to his mother's room.
She pleased him greatly and he was very happy over
her beauty. Soon they celebrated their wedding, and
lived together happily to the end of their lives. Old Abraham lived many years longer with his children. He saw
how dearly they loved each other and was very glad and
contented over it. When he died at a very great age, he
was laid to rest beside Sarah his wife in the cave of
Machpelah which he had bought from the sons of Heth
for four hundred shekels. And there he lies to the
present day.

JACOB AND ESAU

For twenty long years, Isaac and Rebekah lived together, yet never had any children. They were very sad about this, and prayed to God every day that He would send them children. And one fine day, when Isaac was praying to God in one corner of his house and Rebekah in another, beseeching Him to grant their wish, the dear Lord spoke to them and said:

"Two sons will be born to you, and each of them will be the father of a whole nation. The elder will be the stronger, but he will be obliged to serve the younger."

When Isaac and Rebekah heard these words, their hearts were very glad, and they thanked God for His goodness.

Soon afterwards Rebekah gave birth to twins; she named the older brother Esau, and the younger one Jacob.

The two boys were not at all alike. The first-born,

Esau, was strong from birth; his skin was red and covered with hair so that it was almost like a hide. Jacob, however, was delicate and had a smooth body.

When they had grown up, they chose different ways. Esau became a hunter, tramped around in woods and fields, and hunted game; but Jacob was a quiet man, he stayed at home and learned a lot out of books.

Isaac loved Esau the better, because he always prepared tasty food for him from the game he killed. But Rebekah loved the younger son Jacob; it pleased her that he was always reading books and studying earnestly, and she hoped he would some day become a scholar.

It happened one day that Jacob cooked a dish of red lentils, which smelled and tasted very good. In the meantime, Esau came home from the field. He was tired from hunting, and was very hungry. So he asked Jacob to give him some of the dish of lentils.

But Jacob was always jealous of Esau because he was the first-born and answered him:

"I will give you all that I have cooked, but you must sell me your birthright for it."

Esau agreed to this, for his hunger was very great and he wanted the fine lentils very much. So he did not give any thought to it, and with a light heart exchanged his birthright for the dish of lentils. But when he had finished eating, Jacob said to him that his paternal birthright was now gone. Esau was very sorrowful about it, but that did not help him, because what he had promised he also had to keep. However, it served him right, for he had been too thoughtless; he had not valued his birthright enough, and had been too greedy for the lentils. So if today anything like that happens, the proverb still holds true everywhere: "He sold his birthright for a dish of lentils."

ISAAC'S BLESSING

Years had passed by, and Isaac had grown to be an old man. He could no longer see or hear very well, and he felt that his end was near. Then one day he called his son Esau to him and said:

"My son, the spring is here, and every living thing waits for a blessing. Take your bow and arrow, go out into the forest, hunt a wild animal for me and prepare it for food. If I like it, I will bestow upon you before my death the blessing with which my father Abraham blessed me."

But Rebekah was standing behind the door and she heard these words. So she called her son Jacob and said:

"My son, go into the stable and bring me a little goat that I may prepare it for your father to eat, just the way he likes it. When it is ready, you carry it in to him that he may think you are Esau and will bless you before he dies."

Then Jacob said:

"My brother Esau is hairy and rough, and my father will recognize me."

But Rebekah said:

"Cover your hands with hide, so that your father will think you are Esau, and do as I tell you."

Jacob did as Rebekah had ordered him; he killed two small goats and brought them to his mother; she prepared them for food just as his father liked. When it was ready, Jacob put on Esau's best clothes, took the hide and covered his hands with it, as well as the skin around his neck where it was smooth; he hung a bow and arrow on his back and carried Isaac his favorite dish.

"Get up, Father," he said in a disguised voice, "I am bringing you your meat."

But Isaac was surprised that Esau had returned so quickly from the hunt, and asked:

"Have you had luck today at hunting that you have come home so soon?"

"Yes," said Jacob, "God helped me and sent a wild animal in my path."

Then Isaac was pleased at the pious words of his son and said:

"My child, you have become devout; come closer, I want to feel you and see if you are really my son Esau," and when he touched his hands, he said:

"These are the hands of Esau, but the voice is Jacob's. Give me something to eat, my son." Then he ate of the food which Rebekah had prepared for him, and it tasted good to him. When Jacob came near to his father, Isaac noticed the smell of his clothing and said:

"Your clothes smell of the fields, upon which God's blessing rests," and he blessed him with the blessing of his fathers.

Meanwhile Esau roamed around in the forest and hunted after game. At last he caught a fawn and tied it to a tree. Then the devil came along and unbound the animal which quickly ran away. So Esau caught another fawn and tied it likewise to a tree. But the devil unbound that one, too. So it went on until nightfall— whatever Esau caught, the devil set free. It was quite late in the evening when Esau at last killed a wild animal and went home with his game. He quickly prepared his father's favorite dish, took it to him and said:

"Arise, Father, I am bringing you something to eat. And when you have eaten, give me your blessing."

Isaac was much amazed and asked:

"Who are you?"

And Esau answered:

"Don't you know me? I am Esau, your elder son."

Then Isaac was overcome with great trembling and shivering and he cried out:

"Woe is me! Who then was the hunter who brought me the food a little while ago, and to whom I gave the blessing?"

When Esau heard these words, he began to sob and cry; he begged his father that he would bless him also, and he said:

"Have you then only one blessing? Bless me too,

Father! I will not move from this spot until you have given me a blessing likewise."

But Isaac said:

"What shall I do? Jacob was with me and through cunning has stolen away the blessing from me. I have made him lord over you, and all his brothers I have made his servants. I have given him corn and wine, and there is nothing else left for you. Now it must so remain. You will have to live by your sword, and serve your brother. But some day you will set yourself free from your brother and you yourself shall become lord!"

Then Esau said no more, but his heart was filled with hatred. He determined to kill Jacob and thought to himself:

"On the day when my father dies, I will slay my brother."

JACOB'S FLIGHT FROM ESAU

Rebekah was very much afraid that Esau would do some harm to Jacob. Once when she was walking in the field with Jacob she talked with him and said:

"My son, your brother Esau is not kindly disposed toward you; I fear he will do you an injury. Go to my brother Laban and stay there for a while, until Esau's anger is cooled. It is time, too, that you look around for the right woman for yourself; you are now grown up and must get a wife. Maybe the dear Lord will help you to find a woman there who will please you."

When Jacob heard these words, he too became frightened and wanted to run away at once. So Rebekah went to Isaac and begged him to give Jacob a parting blessing. And Isaac let Jacob come to him, became reconciled, gave him his blessing and said:

"I see that you are better than your brother and that it was right for me to give you the blessing of my fathers. May the Lord keep you so that you may become the father of a great and strong people."

But his mother was very sorrowful at the thought of her favorite son going away from her; she got ready a bundle for him to carry on his journey and wept bitterly as she did it. She went with him a little way beyond the city and said to him:

"Do not be afraid, my son, God will help you. Go to my brother, he has beautiful daughters, perhaps one of them will please you. Go, and be of good courage."

In the meantime, Esau came home; he saw that Jacob had gone away and asked about it. The answer he received was that Jacob had gone out into the wide world to seek a wife for himself. When Esau heard this, he also grew eager to marry. He did not think about it very long, but went to Ishmael in the wilderness, took his daughter for a wife, and returned to his father with her.

But Jacob wandered along on his way alone. With the bundle on his back and a staff in his hand, he went through forest and field, over valley and mountain, begging the dear Lord to be with him on his journey. It was nightfall when he came to a place where a great many stones were lying around, and as he was very tired he decided to spend the night there. But because he was afraid of wild animals he took all the stones and piled them around him; he put the biggest stone under his head, arranged a place to rest and lay down. But he had lain there only a little while when the stones began to fight with one another because every one of them wanted to lie under Jacob's head. At first Jacob hadn't the least idea of what all this meant. But when he listened closely, he found out that these were the same stones which his grandfather Abraham had used for the altar when he intended to sacrifice his son Isaac. Then Jacob saw that God had led him to that spot; he felt safe and protected and fell quietly asleep.

And he dreamed that a great ladder stood upon the earth, and the top of it reached to heaven. Angels ascended to heaven upon the ladder and others came down on it to earth. But on the highest rung stood the dear Lord and He said to Jacob:

"I am the God of Abraham and the God of Isaac your father. The whole land which you see around you I will give to you and to your children. I will always be with you and will bless you, so that you will become a great nation. And I will never forsake you, but will do everything which I have promised you."

When Jacob awoke the next morning he was greatly moved; he realized that it was a holy place where he had passed the night, and that the dear Lord meant well by him. He took the stones and laid them one on top of the other, then poured oil on the topmost stone, anointed the place and named it Beth-el, which means the house of God. Then he said:

"Almighty God! If I have understood You rightly, You will always be with me, You will give me bread to eat, clothing to put on, and will lead me back to my parents in peace. If You do this for me, I will build a temple on this spot in Your honor. I and my children will come to You three times each year to bring sacrifices and to serve You, as long as we live."

And Jacob's dream was fulfilled, and the dear Lord bestowed rich blessings upon him. But also what Jacob had said came to pass; for after many long years the building of the temple at Beth-el was begun by David the great King of the Jews, and the wise King Solomon completed it. But when the Babylonians invaded the country, they led the Jews into captivity, destroyed the land and also the magnificent temple at Beth-el. The Jews were captives in Babylonia for seventy years. When they were set free, they built the temple a second time. After that, it stood for five hundred years in Beth-el and all the God-fearing went there to pray to the Lord and to take sacrifices to Him. But again enemies came into the land; this time they were the Romans. They destroyed the temple and only the sacred stones are now left; they lie on the same spot where God appeared to Jacob in a dream. They form a great wall which is called the Wailing Wall. The pious Jews of the whole world assemble there. They light lights in the clefts of the wall, pray to God and pour out to Him their troubles and their distress. I too have been there and I saw the stones with my own eyes: great, four-edged stones. I have lighted a light in the cleft of the wall and have prayed there together with many other Jews.

JACOB AND RACHEL

With a happy heart Jacob left the place where he
had experienced such a wonderful thing and continued
on his way. Toward noon he came to a well. Before the
well lay an enormous stone which first had to be rolled
away so that the sheep could be watered. The stone,
however, was so big and heavy that one man alone
could not lift it. All the shepherds had to be there together, for only all together could they roll the stone
away from the mouth of the well and then after the
sheep had been watered, place it again before the open-
ing. As Jacob came to the well, three shepherds had just
arrived there with their flocks and Jacob said to them:

"Where do you come from, my brothers?"

"From Haran," they answered him.

"Do you know Laban the son of Nahor?" Jacob
asked further.

And they said:

"Yes, we know him; his daughter Rachel comes

every day with her sheep, to water them at the well."

But Jacob wondered why the shepherds did not water their flocks and he asked them:

"Why do you not water your flocks? It will still be daylight for a long while, and you have time enough to work in the field."

Then they told him how heavy the stone was, and that one alone could not lift it. While they were thus talking together, Rachel came to the well with her father's sheep. And the shepherds told him she was Rachel, Laban's daughter. She came lightly along, as if she were playing with the sheep. Her face was illumined by the sun, and Jacob could see how lovely and charming she was. So he went toward her and said:

"Sister, let me water your sheep."

He took hold of the big stone all alone, rolled it away from the well and watered her sheep. Then he went to Rachel, put his arms around her neck, kissed her and wept. Rachel was greatly astonished at this and asked him:

"Why do you cry, shepherd? Who are you? Where do you come from? And why have you been so good to me?"

Then Jacob said:

"I am Jacob, the son of Isaac, and my mother Rebekah is your father's sister."

Then Rachel was greatly pleased with him, and begged him to go to her father's house.

But the shepherds saw what had taken place, and could not trust their eyes; they were astonished at the stranger and admired his strength.

Rachel ran home quickly, and told her father that Jacob had arrived. Then Laban came to meet Jacob, greeted and embraced him, and was pleased over his fine guest. Also he hoped in his secret heart that Jacob had brought with him just as many handsome presents as once Eliezer had done, and gold and silver from his father, for he knew that Isaac was rich.

Jacob thanked Laban for his hospitality and said:

"My dear friends, I have brought nothing with me but my staff and my bundle."

Then Laban made a sour face and said:

"You are of our kinship, and will stay with us for a while."

But Jacob said:

"I will not eat your bread for nothing; I will work for you and tend your flocks."

Then Laban asked him:

"What wages do you want?"

"Your daughter Rachel pleases me very much. She was the first one to meet me and was kind to me. I will gladly serve you seven years for her, because I love her."

Laban was satisfied with that. And Jacob entered into his service. Jacob served seven long years for Rachel and it seemed to him as if it were only seven days, so dearly did he love her.

HOW LABAN DECEIVED JACOB

Jacob served for Rachel seven long years; he was faithful to Laban and took care of his flocks as if they were his own. If one little lamb ever wandered away, he would go out in the fields to search for it, and would not come back until he had found it. If ever a little lamb grew sick and could not go along with the flock, he took it in his arms and carried it home. He never set the dog on the sheep; a gentle call was always enough to make them follow him. Day and night he was at work and he did not fear the cutting cold of the night nor the blazing heat of the day. But Rachel came out to him every day in the fields. There they sat and talked together and counted the months, weeks and days which yet must pass before their wedding. They were very gay; they laughed and sang, and rejoiced in their youth and their love.

But one day Rachel came to Jacob in the field, sat

down beside him and did not say a word. Then Jacob said to her:

"What is the matter with you, my dear little bride? Why are you so sad? Has something bad happened to you?"

"My darling," answered Rachel, "I must tell you of something dreadful. I realized, at the door of my parents' room, that they were talking about me; then I listened and I heard them discussing how they could arrange to give you my sister Leah instead of me for a wife. They want very much to marry her off first, because she is older than I am and not pretty, and it might be impossible afterwards to find another suitor for her."

Then Jacob said:

"I don't love your elder sister, and I don't want to marry her. It is for you that I have worked and you must become my wife."

Then Rachel took courage and said:

"I'll tell you, Jacob, we will agree upon a sign. When my mother leads me to the marriage ceremony and, covered with the bridal veil, I am standing at your side, you must ask me very softly: 'Is it you, my dear bride?' And I will answer you: 'It is I, my beloved Jacob.' And you will recognize me by my voice."

"Good," said Jacob, "that's settled. But if it's not you, I will not let myself be wedded to another."

When the seven years had finally come to an end, Jacob went to Laban and said: "Give me Rachel for my wife; the seven years are now over and I have served you faithfully for her."

Then Laban acted as if he were agreed to it; the

day of the wedding was fixed and was to be celebrated with pomp and splendor.

But on the wedding day, their mother did not bring Rachel into the room, but Leah; she put fine linen on her and clothing of silk and velvet. And Rachel thought to herself: "Adorn yourself and make yourself as beautiful as you can, my lover will soon recognize you anyway."

However when the hour for the wedding arrived, Rachel felt very sorry for her sister. She saw Leah's joy and she did not have the heart to cause her grief and shame. So she told her about the agreement with Jacob and said:

"When Jacob asks you: 'Is it you, Rachel, my dear bride?' keep still. I will answer him in your stead."

With that she fondled and kissed her sister and did not show how sad she felt. At the ceremony Rachel stood close behind Leah, so that she could answer Jacob's question. And Jacob asked very softly:

"Are you Rachel, my dear bride?"

Then Rachel said behind Leah's back, just as softly:

"Yes, it is I, my beloved Jacob."

But Jacob asked her again:

"Why is your voice so sad, my dear bride?"

"I am praying to God," replied Rachel, "that He may bestow His blessing upon us."

And Jacob said:

"Don't worry, my love, God will give us His blessing."

Then Rachel grew still more sorrowful and she

wept; but only very softly, so that Jacob could not hear it.

The wedding ceremony was ended, and Leah became Jacob's wife. When the marriage feast was over and Leah was alone with her husband, he took off her veil and realized that he had married not Rachel but Leah. Then he flew into a rage, ran to Laban and said:

"Why did you do this to me? Did I not serve you for Rachel? Why have you deceived me?"

"It is not the custom in our land," replied Laban, "that the younger daughter should be married before the older one. Keep Leah, be kind and loving to her and I will give you Rachel for a wife also, although you must serve me another seven years for her."

Jacob was agreed to that, because he loved Rachel with his whole heart and did not want to live without her.

When Laban saw that Jacob was good and kind to Leah, he did not delay very long, and gave him Rachel to be his wife also. Then Jacob had two wives. But you do not need to be surprised about that, because in those days it was still the custom for a man to have several wives.

JACOB'S FLIGHT FROM LABAN

Jacob lived for many years with his two wives and was good to both of them. But he loved Rachel a thousand times more than Leah. Then the dear Lord had pity on Leah and sent her four sons as consolation. The oldest son was called Reuben, the second one Simeon, the third Levi—he afterwards became the most pious of them all—and the fourth was Judah. He was the strongest and the most courageous and the Hebrew kings descended from him.

But Rachel had no children and was very sad about it. She would gladly have given up her beauty if God had sent her a child instead. She prayed day and night and implored God to give her a child. The dear Lord heard her supplication and she had a son whom she named Joseph. He was the handsomest creature in the world.

Jacob was a good father; he was very happy over his children and loved them tenderly. And when they were grown he often took all of them with him into the field. Then they sat down on the ground around him and he would tell them a great many things about the dear Lord. And in the night when the sky was dark and the stars shone and glittered, he would lie down with them, so that they could look up into the stars, and he would tell them all about their grandfather Abraham, how wise he was, and how he had found the true God, —about Noah, who built the ark, and about Adam and Eve. He also taught them early how to look after sheep, because he wanted to make good shepherds out of them. So things went along year in, year out, until the other seven years, which Jacob had to serve for Rachel, were past.

Then Jacob went to Laban, talked with him and said:

"I have served you long enough for your two daughters. It is time that I look out for my children. Give me my wives and my children and let me depart into my own country."

Laban did not want to do that, because he knew very well that it would not be easy for him to find another shepherd as good as Jacob, and he said:

"I will not let you go. God has blessed me because of you, and in the time during which you have been with me my wealth has increased; my flocks pasture all over the land. Name your own wages; I will give you everything that you demand, but you must remain with me."

Then Jacob acted as if he were agreed to Laban's plan and he said:

"Today I will go through your flocks and I will sort

out all the spotted and speckled sheep for you. The sheep which from now on are born spotted and speckled shall be my property. If you are willing to do this, I will go on serving you and tending your flocks."

Laban was agreed, and Jacob stayed in his service.

And when the time came that the sheep had little lambs, they all had red and black speckles. Laban, however, envied Jacob such rich possessions and he said:

"I have pondered over the matter. I will give you the white sheep; the flecked and spotted ones shall belong to me."

But what did the dear Lord do? When the time came that the sheep again had young ones, they were all white, so that Jacob's flocks became very large and he had to take on a strange shepherd to help him, for he could no longer manage the work alone. He let his children tend his own flocks while he took care of Laban's himself.

But Laban's children were very jealous of Jacob, they envied him his rich possessions and they said among themselves that Jacob had stolen from Laban. Then Jacob told both his wives to come to him and he said to them:

"Your father's children are going around with anger in their hearts toward me and they are telling everywhere that I have stolen from Laban. I have served fourteen years for the two of you, and it is now time that I look after our children. God has shown himself to me and has commanded me to depart into the land of my fathers."

And he asked them if they wished to go with him. Then they answered him:

"Take us with you, for nothing any longer keeps us in the house of our father. He has sold us and he himself fixed the price. Do as God has said unto you."

So Jacob arose, placed his wives and his children upon camels, got all his belongings together, and in the dead of night when everything was wrapt in deep sleep, he left Mesopotamia and set out on his way to Canaan, the land of his fathers.

This all happened at a time when Laban had gone away from home to shear his sheep. Meanwhile he came back with his flocks and found that Jacob and his family had departed, also that his idols were missing, and he believed that Jacob had stolen them from him. Then he grew terribly angry, called his brothers to help him and pursued Jacob and his family in hot haste. Six days and nights he followed after him, and could not overtake him. But on the way the dear Lord appeared to Laban in the night and warned him to do no harm to Jacob. Finally on the evening of the seventh day Laban saw fire on the Mount of Gilead, and soon he recognized Jacob's camp. He at once went up the mountain and pitched his tent there. Then he talked with Jacob and said:

"What have you done to me? Why have you deceived me and led my daughters away as if you had taken them captive in war? Why did you say nothing to me and steal away from me unawares? I would have accompanied you with song and music, with drums and harps. Why did you rob me of my idols? I have strength enough to revenge myself upon you, but the God of your fathers has revealed Himself to me and has commanded me to spare you."

Then Jacob said:

"I fled away from you secretly because you would not have allowed me to depart in peace. You would not have given me your daughters, and they themselves begged me to take them along. But I have not stolen your gods from you. Go and seek, and the one with whom you find them, he shall die."

Then Laban went into Jacob's tent, into Leah's and into the two maidservants', but he did not find the idols. At last he went into Rachel's tent. But Rachel, who had really taken the images away with her, hid them in the saddle and sat upon it herself. When her father entered her tent, she asked him to excuse her for remaining seated, as she felt rather weak and could not get up. So Laban did not find the idols, though he hunted for them diligently

They argued for a while longer, and reproached each other bitterly, until finally all the men who were gathered around them said Jacob was right. At last Laban realized that he had done wrong. He wished to become reconciled with Jacob, and said to his brothers: "Take some stones and pile them in a heap," and he himself laid the first stone. Then they did as he had commanded them, and soon a whole mountain was standing before them. It was to be witness of the peace between Laban and Jacob. After that they ate and drank together and stayed on the mountain overnight. The next morning they said good-bye to each other and departed in peace, each one his own way.

JACOB'S MEETING WITH ESAU

The nearer Jacob came to his native land, the oftener was he forced to think of his brother Esau from whom he once had fled. His heart grew anxious and he was very frightened at the thought of meeting his brother. So he sent messengers to him and ordered them to say that he was returning from a strange country to his native land. It was not long till the messengers came back and said that Esau was coming to meet Jacob with four hundred men. Then Jacob was greatly distressed because he thought that Esau was going to overpower him. So he divided all the people who were with him into two camps, for he thought: "If Esau falls upon the one, the other in the meantime may escape." Then he prayed to God and said:

"Almighty God, I am unworthy of all the mercies which You have bestowed upon me. Lonely and poor, with only a staff in my hand, and a bundle on my back, I left my father's house; rich and laden with possessions I return. In this hour also stand by me, and save me from the vengeance of my brother."

Then he chose the finest cattle in his herds and sent them as a present to Esau, for he thought to himself: "Perhaps his anger will be calmed and he will spare us." He took his wives and his children and crossed over the pond which lay in their path. On the opposite bank, however, he noticed that his earthen pots were missing. He was very sorry about it, for he had been forced to work so hard for everything; so he went back again to get them. In the meantime the night had fallen, and out of the darkness a strange man appeared who fell upon Jacob and wrestled with him the whole night. However, he could not overcome him and at last he said:

"Let me go."

But Jacob answered:

"I will not let you go until you tell me who you are."

And the man said:

"What does it matter to you who I am? I can't tell you that. But I will say this to you: In your lifetime you have struggled with men and have overpowered them; now you have wrestled with one of God's angels and have vanquished him also. Therefore you shall no longer be called Jacob, but Israel, the warrior of God." After that he blessed Jacob and disappeared.

Then Jacob realized that God was gracious to him and his anxiety was lessened.

When the day dawned, Jacob saw that his brother Esau was approaching with the four hundred men. He hurried to his family and divided them into three groups: first came the handmaidens with their children, then Leah with hers, and at the last Rachel with Joseph. Jacob himself stood at the very front and thus they awaited Esau.

But when Esau caught sight of Jacob, he ran forward and embraced him. And Jacob said:

"Brother Esau, why are you coming toward me with men and swords? I come with wives and children and I bring along also oxen, cattle and sheep which I have not taken from our father, for I left behind all our father's possessions for you. Everything that I bring with me I have earned through my own effort and I have worked twenty years for it."

Then Esau answered:

"Brother Jacob, I am not thinking of any warfare with you. For twenty years I did not see you, and then I heard that you were coming home. So I arose and marched toward you."

So Jacob's heart was stirred; he fell again into his brother's arms and they wept for joy.

Then Jacob showed his brother his wives and children, and Esau was greatly pleased with them.

As they now wished to go farther, Jacob said:

"My brother, you go on before us. I have with me children of tender age and suckling lambs; haste might do them harm."

Then they said good-bye to each other and departed in peace, each his own way. Esau went home, but Jacob went to Shechem, bought land and settled there with his family. And as he had prospered well, he remembered the vow which he once had made at Beth-el. He called his sons to him, told them to put on their best garments, and they all went together to Beth-el. There they poured oil over the stones, prayed to God, brought sacrifices to Him and thanked Him for all His goodness.

RACHEL'S DEATH

At this time Rachel bore her second son and they named him Benjamin. But soon afterwards she grew very ill and died. Jacob was deeply grieved over this, because you of course know how dearly he loved her. He wanted to bury his beloved Rachel in the cave of Machpelah where Abraham and Sarah, and Isaac and Rebekah were laid to rest. But God said to Jacob:

"Do not bury her in the tomb of your fathers, bury her on the road to the Euphrates in Bethlehem. When the people of Israel are some day driven out of their country, the fugitives will have to pass Rachel's tomb. Then Rachel will rise from her grave, she will come to me and will implore me for pity upon her children, and she will say: 'You remember how I sacrificed myself for my sister when I was to be married to my beloved Jacob? Is this the reward for my children?' And I will listen to her pleading."

In the Holy Word, the following lines are written concerning this:

"In the times of distress, when the people of Israel will be stricken down by misfortune a voice of mourning will be heard from Rachel's tomb. The voice of Rachel weeping for her children."

And there Rachel lies to the present day. Over her grave a little shrine now stands. Inside it many lights burn, for every pilgrim on his way to Jerusalem, also visits Rachel's tomb, and lights a little light in her honor. I have been there too and have kindled a light to honor Rachel.

DINA

Jacob lived in Shechem a long time and was a rich man and highly esteemed. His sheep and cattle were well fed, his possessions grew from day to day, and he could undertake whatever he wished; everything turned out well, for the dear Lord always stood by him. But Jacob had in addition to his twelve sons an only daughter, named Dina, who was a very beautiful girl. She often went for a walk in the city; then she would put on her prettiest clothes and would adorn herself, for it gave her pleasure when the people looked after her in amazement and praised her beauty.

It happened one day that the king's son caught sight of her. He was at once enkindled with ardent love for her and wanted to have her for a wife. So he approached her secretly, carried her away to his castle and hid her inside it. Then he went to his father and begged him to make Dina his wife, and the king was agreed.

When Jacob received the news that Dina had been carried off by the son of the king of Shechem he said nothing, for he wanted to wait until his sons had come back from the fields.

King Hamor, the father of the young prince, was however very much afraid of the sons of Jacob. So he went to Jacob and said:

"My son has carried away your daughter. Forgive him because he is young and foolhardy, and he loves her very much. I have come to you to implore you to give your child to my son for a wife. I am rich. All that I have will some day belong to my son, and Dina will be queen in my country."

Thereupon Jacob answered him:

"You know that we are Jews. If you also will become Jews, then I will give my daughter to your son for a wife."

With that the old king was satisfied and turned back to Shechem.

Soon afterwards Jacob's sons came from the fields, and when they heard what injury the young king's son had done to them, they swore vengeance upon the young man and upon the whole city of Shechem. Simeon and Levi, the two strongest among them, rushed upon the city and killed all the men and boys. They took all the possessions which they could carry away with them and they brought back Dina to their father.

When Jacob saw what had happened, he was filled with great anxiety and said:

"What have you done? You have brought misfortune upon me and I cannot stay in this land any longer.

They will all march against us now, all who belong to the country, and they will destroy us."

But his sons answered:

"What did you want us to do? We had to avenge our sister and that is what we have done. We are afraid of nothing, let the enemy come."

Then Jacob saw how strong and brave his sons were, and that he could depend upon them.—But no enemy arose against Jacob and his sons, for they were famed far and wide because of their strength, and everybody was afraid to fight with them.

JOSEPH AND HIS BROTHERS

Jacob loved Joseph the best of all his sons. Joseph's brothers had to do heavy work and look after the flocks the whole day long, while Joseph stayed at home with his father. Jacob gave him beautiful silken garments, but the other sons had to wear the usual woolen clothing. So Joseph grew haughty and very proud toward his brothers. He kept himself aloof from them, and preferred to stay with the children of Bilha, his mother's maid, because they always flattered him. Moreover, his brothers knew that he carried evil gossip about them to their father; so they hated him and bore malice in their hearts toward him.

One fine morning Joseph said to his brothers:

"Last night I had a remarkable dream. I dreamed that we all had been binding sheaves in the field, and my sheaf arose and stood up high, but your sheaves bowed low before it."

Another time he came to his brothers and told

them he had dreamed that the sun, the moon and eleven stars bowed themselves before him, and that he thought it meant his father and mother and his eleven brothers.

Then Jacob grew angry, he scolded Joseph for such overbearing words, and said:

"What kind of talk is that? It may come to pass that I and your brothers shall bow down before you. But certainly not your Mother! For she is dead!"

But in his heart he was very happy over this dream and wished it might be fulfilled, for he loved Joseph fervently. But the brothers hated Joseph more than ever before, they laughed and jeered at him, and called him the dreamer.

Joseph's brothers lived in the valley of Hebron, but they pastured their flocks near Shechem. It happened once that they did not come home for a long time. Then Jacob was filled with anxiety over them and said to Joseph:

"Go, my son, to Shechem and inquire after your brothers. I should like to know also how the sheep are coming along."

So Joseph arose and went to Shechem. But when he arrived there, his brothers were not to be found and he did not know where to turn his steps. Then a man came walking along whom he asked:

"Have you not seen my brothers? They are the sons of Jacob and ought to be tending their flocks here."

And the man told him that his brothers had gone toward Dothan. So Joseph went to Dothan to search for his brothers and he found them there. When the brothers saw Joseph coming toward them, they said to one another:

"Here comes our dreamer. We are all alone with him here and we'll now get even with him."

And they decided to kill him.

Reuben however had pity on Joseph; he wanted to save him from the hands of his brothers and said:

"Brothers, we do not want to murder him. It would be better for us to throw him into a pit. Our hands shall then not be stained with his blood."

This advice pleased the brothers very much and they decided to follow it. When Joseph came, they took him into their midst, stripped off his silken coat, and threw him into a pit. The pit was deep, but it had no water in it. Joseph only hurt himself in falling, but he remained alive.

One of the brothers had to go every day to their father to look after him. When Reuben's turn came, he wanted to take Joseph out of the pit and carry him away; however, he did not succeed with this plan for his brothers surrounded the pit and kept watch there by day and by night. And Reuben had to go to his father without Joseph.—Judah was now the head in his place, because it was agreed among them that every day a different one should become the head, and all the brothers then had to obey him. After Reuben had gone away, they all sat down around the pit, ate and drank and paid no attention to Joseph, who lay bruised at the bottom of the pit, and was crying bitterly.

Then a caravan came along the way. They were merchants from Gilead who carried spices, balm and myrrh upon their camels and were going down to Egypt. And Judah said to his brothers:

"Brothers, what good will it do us if we kill Joseph and stain our hands with his blood? It will be better for us to sell him to these people."

That contented the brothers. They called to the merchants, pulled Joseph out of the pit and offered him for sale.

"What price do you demand?" asked the merchants.

"Twenty pieces of silver," answered the brothers.

Then the merchants counted out the required price and took Joseph along with them to Egypt. The brothers divided the money among themselves.

In the meantime, Reuben came back, and when he found that Joseph was no longer in the pit he was filled with despair and cried out:

"Brothers, what have you done? The boy is no longer there! Where shall I go? What can I say to our father?"

Then the brothers went off and killed a kid; with their own teeth they tore Joseph's coat in pieces and dipped it in the animal's blood.

The father had been standing a long time at the window, watching restlessly for his sons, because his heart told him something had gone wrong. When they came, he searched among them for Joseph, but found him not. Then the sons showed him the bloody rags, and said that Joseph must have been torn to pieces by wild animals. When Jacob heard this message he tore his garments, put on sackcloth and cried like a little child. Then the sons were very sorry over their wicked deed; but they could not tell their father the truth because they had previously given one another the promise not to tell the secret. They threw themselves on their knees before him, kissed his hands and tried to comfort him. But Jacob did not hear their consoling words, because his heart was full of sorrow. For days and nights he sat on the ground and wept for his favorite son.

JOSEPH IN EGYPT

Listen now to what in the meantime happened to Joseph. The merchants from Gilead took him to Egypt and offered him for sale in the market-place. Potiphar, the Master of the Horse to the King of Egypt bought Joseph as a slave. Joseph went to Potiphar's house and at first was simply a servant. That was very hard for him because his father had never made him work. But he pulled himself together, was industrious, willing and polite, so that he soon won the approval of his master and received advancement. It was not long until Potiphar noticed how smart and ready Joseph was, and also that he understood a great deal which the others did not know; so he gave him his complete confidence. He delivered to him the keys of his treasury, and made him overseer of his entire household.

But Joseph was such a handsome young man that every one was astonished at his good looks. Once Potiphar's wife told her women-friends that she had a servant of unusual beauty. The women, however, were not willing to believe her. So Potiphar's wife invited her friends to see her, had them sit in patriarchal chairs and feasted them with lovely apples. While they were peeling their apples, she called Joseph into the room. Joseph entered and he was so handsome that the women could not speak for amazement. They were charmed with his beauty, and could not turn their eyes away from him. And as they were still peeling their apples, they cut their fingers and peeled off their own skin, also.

But Joseph grew very proud and conceited and soon he had nothing in his mind but dress and vanity. Also he no longer thought of his sorrowing father. Joseph's behavior displeased the dear Lord, and He decided to punish him for his conceit and lack of affection. He allowed Potiphar's wife to be enkindled with ardent love for Joseph. She lay in wait for him everywhere, gave him no rest, and urged him to kill Potiphar and take her for his wife. But Joseph refused to do this, because he was an honest young man and faithful to his master.

"How can I betray my lord?" he said to Potiphar's wife. "He has conferred so much favor upon me and has made me overseer of his whole house, and has given his possessions into my care. Shall this then be my thanks? No, I will not do it!"

Then Potiphar's wife grew very afraid that Joseph would betray her to her husband, so she went in secret to Potiphar and told him that his servant Joseph was in love with her and wanted to have her for his wife; that he followed her continually and tried to persuade her that she should kill her husband. With these wicked words she poisoned Potiphar's mind, and he ordered Joseph thrown into prison. Thus was Joseph punished by the Lord.

JOSEPH IN PRISON

When Joseph sat in prison, God again bestowed
His mercy upon him. The keeper of the dungeon found
pleasure in him and put him in charge of the prison-
ers.— It happened at the same time that the chief baker
and the chief cupbearer of King Pharaoh were serving
sentences in prison for having given offense to the King.
The baker was being punished because three dead flies
had been found in the bread which was intended for the
royal table; and the cupbearer because, in the goblet
which he had handed to the king, three flies had likewise
been found.

As Joseph entered their cell one morning he saw
that they both were very sad; so he asked:

"Why are you so sorrowful?"

And they answered him:

"We have had unusual dreams and we do not know
what they mean."

"Well," said Joseph, "tell me your dreams, perhaps I can explain them to you."

Then the cupbearer began thus:

"I dreamed that I stood before a grape-vine. The vine had three branches, they grew and blossomed and their clusters of grapes ripened. But I held Pharaoh's goblet in my hand, took the grapes and pressed them into the cup and I gave it to Pharaoh."

Then Joseph said to him:

"The three branches are three days. In three days Pharaoh will deliver you from prison and will put you back in your former office. But when you come before Pharaoh think of me, and attend to it that I too am set free, for I was stolen away in secret from the land of the Jews and I have done no wrong here; in spite of that I have been imprisoned."

When the baker heard how well Joseph had interpreted the dream of the cupbearer, he began also to tell his:

"I dreamed that I was carrying three baskets of baked goods on my head, and in the uppermost one was the best and finest things that were baked. Then a flock of birds came flying and ate up everything that was in the basket."

Thereupon Joseph said:

"The three baskets mean likewise three days. In three days Pharaoh will have you hanged on a gallows and the birds will devour your body."

Three days later Pharaoh celebrated his birthday, and he gave a great feast to his laborers and servants. The cupbearer and the baker were taken out of the prison and they were tried in public. The cupbearer had to defend himself first. He said:

"In the moment when the unfortunate accident happened, I was holding the cup in one hand and pouring in the wine with the other. So I could not prevent the flies from falling into the cup."

This explanation was very satisfactory to Pharaoh. They freed the cupbearer of the crime and put him back in his same office. Then the chief baker's turn came. He, however, could not plead anything as an excuse, for the flies had fallen into the dough while he was kneading it, so that he might have been able to take them out. Hence his guilt was clear and he was condemned to death. On the very same day Pharaoh had him hanged on the gallows and the birds ate up his body. So both dreams were fulfilled as Joseph had interpreted them.

JOSEPH IS MADE RULER OVER EGYPT

Two years later it happened that Pharaoh had a dream: he stood by the river Nile and saw seven cows come up out of the water; they were fat and fine looking, and they went into the grass to graze. After them he saw again seven other cows come up out of the same water; they were ugly and very thin. The lean cows ran after the others, fell upon them and ate them completely up. But strange to say: it could not be noticed. For afterwards they remained just as thin as before.

Then Pharaoh awoke. But he soon fell into another deep sleep. He dreamed again, and saw seven ears of corn which were full and fine-grained, and they grew up out of one stalk. And after that he saw seven ears which were parched and empty. And behold! the poor ears devoured the thick full ones; but no one could notice it for they stayed just as withered as before.

Pharaoh awoke and realized that this also had

been a dream. But he could not fall asleep again because the dreams gave him no peace. He tried as hard as he could, but he did not know how to explain them.

When it was morning, Pharaoh sent his people after the great fortune-tellers of the land and the interpreters of dreams; and when they came he related his dreams to them and begged them to explain their meaning. They listened to him carefully, shook their wise heads and were silent for a long time. Then they did much debating, and each one said something different. One thought the seven fat cows meant seven daughters who were to be born to Pharaoh, and that the seven lean ones indicated that these daughters should die. Another one asserted, on the other hand, that the seven fat cows meant seven battles which Pharaoh was to win, the seven thin ones, seven battles which he would lose. But then a third one asked how they could explain that the seven fat cows were eaten up by the seven thin ones, and no one knew how to answer him.

All of these interpretations displeased Pharaoh. He sent all the wise men away and fell into deep melancholy.

Then the chief cupbearer remembered the young Hebrew Joseph who was still in prison and he went to Pharaoh, threw himself on his knees before him and said:

"My great King, I remember today my sins. Pharaoh was once very angry with his servants and had me thrown into prison together with the chief baker. We dreamed in the same night very unusual things and we did not know how to explain them. At the same time a Hebrew youth, servant to the king's Master of the Horse, was serving a sentence in prison. We told our dreams to him, and just as he explained them to us, so have they also come to pass."

When Pharaoh heard these words, he at once gave the order to free Joseph from his imprisonment, and to lead him before his presence. So Joseph was brought out of the prison. He was washed, dressed in other clothing and taken in unto Pharaoh. The king sat upon his golden throne, and around him the great and the wise men of the land were assembled. Pharaoh's throne had seventy steps. On the first step stood those wise ones who knew only one language; upon the second, those who knew two languages, and so it went on to the last step. Upon the seventieth step Pharaoh sat alone, because he was the only one who understood all seventy languages which are spoken in the world. When Joseph appeared before Pharaoh, the wise men asked him:

"Tell us, how many languages do you understand so that we may assign you your place?"

"I must stand on the seventieth step," replied Joseph, "for I understand seventy languages."

And Joseph spoke the truth, for in the night an angel had come to him and had taught him all seventy tongues.

So Pharaoh beckoned to him graciously, and Joseph stood near him on the seventieth step. The king then told him his dream and begged him to interpret it to him.—Joseph meditated a long while; then he said:

"Mighty Pharaoh! It belongs to God alone to interpret your dream for you. He will do it through me."

Such words pleased Pharaoh greatly and he made a sign to Joseph that he should speak further. And Joseph continued:

"Both of Pharaoh's dreams have the same meaning. God is making known to Pharaoh what He intends to do. The seven fat cows are seven good years just the same as the seven full ears of corn. The seven lean cows, however, are seven bad years, just like the seven parched ears. At first seven years of plenty will come to the land of Egypt, and the land will bear rich fruits and will yield good harvests. After that, there will follow seven years of famine which will lay waste the land and consume the wealth. And because Pharaoh has dreamed his dream twice it is a sign that God has definitely settled upon this plan and that it will soon come to pass." And Joseph advised Pharaoh to select a wise and sensible man, who should take care that during the seven years of plenty a supply of grain should be stored up in the granaries of Egypt for the seven years of famine.

These words pleased Pharaoh and all the people assembled with him and they all agreed together that Joseph himself was the wisest and most sensible man in the land. The king raised him to be the first man in Egypt and said to him:

"From now on you shall stand over every one who is in my house. All the people shall obey you; only the throne shall exalt me above you."

When he had thus spoken, he took the ring from his own hand and placed it on Joseph's finger, he hung a golden chain around his neck, and presented him with magnificent garments. Then he had him seated in his second chariot and driven through all the streets of the city; before him went the cry: "This man is ruler of the land."

Joseph was only thirty years old when he came into this honor and was made to rule over all Egypt. Soon he married a royal princess and his wife gave him two sons. He named the elder Manasseh, which means: "God has blessed me for all the wrongs I have suffered." To the second he gave the name Ephraim, which means: "God has made me to be great in the land of my affliction."

THE BROTHERS IN EGYPT

Everything came to pass exactly as Joseph had prophesied. The next seven years were rich and fruitful, and throughout the whole kingdom the earth gave fruit in great abundance. Joseph sent forth the command that all the grain should be collected in Pharaoh's storehouses, and so much was stored up that it could no longer be measured.

But the seven years of plenty came to an end and the time of famine set in. The earth was dry. If people sowed seed in the soil, the wind carried the seed away, and the earth yielded nothing. The trees were stripped of leaves and there was no fruit in all the land.

All the people suffered hunger; they moaned and cried out to Pharaoh and begged him for bread. But Pharaoh said to the Egyptians who came to him: "Go unto Joseph, and do what he tells you to do." Then they all came to Joseph. And Joseph opened the storehouses of the land and sold grain to the Egyptians at a low cost.

But the famine raged not only in Egypt,—it had spread over all lands, so that people everywhere suffered hunger. Soon people far and wide learned that there was a wise man in Egypt who in the seven years of plenty had collected a great deal of grain, had piled it up in storehouses, and was now selling it. Then they arose and went to Egypt, in order to get grain there for themselves.

The land of Canaan also, where Jacob lived with his children, was suffering from the famine, and the time was drawing near when there would be nothing more left to eat. One day Jacob said to his sons:

"I hear that in the land of Egypt there is cheap grain for sale. Do not tarry but go at once, for otherwise all of us here will starve to death."

Then they took big sacks and plenty of money with them and departed for Egypt.

Jacob sent ten of his sons to Egypt, but Benjamin, Joseph's brother, he kept at home because he was afraid that some accident might happen to him on the way. Also he did not want to allow him to go away from him because, after Joseph, he loved him the best of all his sons, and could not live without him, for of course Benjamin was also his beloved Rachel's son.

But Joseph knew that in the land of Canaan, also, there was no bread, and he thought to himself that his brothers would come to Egypt in order to buy grain. He issued a command by which every stranger who wished to come into the city was compelled to give a ticket upon which his name was written. At nightfall all the tickets were brought to him in his home, because he wanted to find out if his brothers were not among the new arrivals. And one fine day he read upon a ticket: "Reuben, the son of Jacob, has come into the city through the South gate." Then again on another ticket: "Simeon, the son of Jacob, came into the city through the North gate." Thus he found all the ten tickets of his ten brothers, who each had arrived through a different gate because they did not want to cause any sensation. Then he ordered all the granaries locked, except just a single one, and at this one Joseph himself stood to give out the grain.

It was not long until the sons of Jacob came with their camels. Joseph recognized them at once, and his heart began to beat; but he controlled himself, acted like a stranger to them, and asked in a stern voice:

"Who are you?"

And they answered:

"We have come from the land of Canaan to buy grain."

But Joseph said to them:

"You are spies, and you have come to find out where the land is open."

So the brothers answered:

"No, gracious lord, we are not spies, we are quiet, respectable people."

Then Joseph turned to his servants and said:

"Give me my magic cup."

And they brought it to him. It was however just a very ordinary cup, only Joseph acted as if it were a magic one. He took it in his hand, struck against it, then listened carefully a while to the sound and said:

"My magic cup tells me that two of you destroyed a whole city."

Then they turned pale and said:

"Which of us was it?"

So Joseph struck the cup again, listened a while to the sound and pointed to Simeon and Levi.

Then they said:

"In fact we did destroy a city out of revenge for the shame which was done to our sister. But we came here to buy bread. We are twelve sons of an honest old man. The youngest has stayed at home with our father. And one is no longer with us."

But Joseph asked again:

"And what happened to your brother of whom you say that he is no longer with you?"

"He is dead," they answered him.

Then once again Joseph put the magic cup to his ear and said:

"What you say is a lie, for my magic cup tells me that your brother lives; but you sold him for twenty pieces of silver. Is that true?"

Then they dropped their heads very low and were silent.

But Joseph said:

"Fill your sacks with grain, go home to your father and bring me back your youngest brother. One of you I will hold here as a pledge, so that you do what I tell you. Bring him with you that I may see if you have spoken the truth, and then I will allow you to depart in peace."

He demanded this, because he wanted to see his brother Benjamin.

Then Jacob's sons said to one another:

"Now the punishment is falling upon us for having sinned against our brother Joseph. We paid no attention to his tears and had no pity upon him. We sold him like an animal to a strange people. It serves us right that we are to be punished."

When Joseph heard these words he could no longer control his emotion, tears filled his eyes, so that he had to turn away for fear some one would notice. Then again he pulled himself together and had Simeon seized, for he wanted to keep him as a pledge. Thereupon he gave the command that the brothers' sacks should be filled with grain and that their money with which they had paid for the grain should be placed again in the sacks. He also ordered food and drink to be given them to take along on their journey. The brothers loaded the sacks upon their camels and rode away. It was not long until they arrived at a place of shelter. There one of them opened up his sack, to take out some food for the camels, and he found the money lying on the top. He was very much astonished at that, ran in haste to his brothers and told them about it. They were greatly frightened, because they did not know who could have done such a thing, and they felt very anxious for fear they would be blamed in Egypt for being robbers.

THE RETURN OF THE BROTHERS
TO CANAAN

When Joseph's brothers returned home, they told
their father all that had happened to them in Egypt.
They spoke of the great man who had treated them so
ill and had accused them of being spies, of Simeon who
had stayed behind chained in a prison, and finally of
the man's request that Benjamin should be brought to
Egypt. Jacob listened to them silently, but when they
had got to the end of their story he said:

"Let things happen as they may—I will not give
Benjamin to you. Rachel gave me only two children,
one of them I lost years ago, and now shall the other one
be taken from me? No, I will not let him go!"

Then Reuben said to him:

"Father, if I do not bring Benjamin back to you
my own two sons shall die. Trust him to my care!"

But Jacob said:

"You are a fool; are your children then not my

children? What can it profit me if your children also die? It stands as I have said: I will not give you Benjamin."

Not long afterwards, however, all the grain was eaten up and a new supply had to be obtained. Then Jacob again spoke to his sons:

"How did the man happen to say to you that you had one other brother?"

And they answered him:

"We did not tell him about it, but he knew it himself, because he owned a magic cup which told him everything he wanted to know. Hence we had to tell him so that he would see we were speaking the truth."

Then Judah stepped up to his father and said:

"Father, give Benjamin into my keeping. I will answer to you for him with my life. Demand him again from my hands. Without him I will not come into your presence."

Then Jacob saw that he could rely upon Judah, because Judah was the wisest and strongest of his sons and so he entrusted Benjamin to him. He gave them presents to take with them for the great man in Egypt, and he bestowed upon them his fatherly blessing. And they arose and set out with their brother Benjamin for Egypt.

BENJAMIN IN EGYPT

One fine day Joseph saw from afar his brothers arriving. So he ordered sheep to be killed and a special meal to be prepared, for he wanted to receive them in splendor. But the brothers still were constantly afraid that they might be accused in Egypt of robbery, and they said to the servants that Joseph sent out to meet them:

"We found in our sacks the money with which we had paid for the grain, and we have brought it back to you."

Thereupon Joseph's servants answered them:

"You needn't worry yourselves about that; God himself gave the money back to you. We are to lead you to Joseph for he wishes to have you eat with him."

Then the servants washed their hands and feet for them, dressed them in fresh clothes and took them to Joseph. He welcomed them heartily and asked:

"How is your old father getting along? Is he still living?"

And they answered:

"Yes, he is living; he sent you his greetings and told us to give you these gifts."

Joseph was very pleased and thanked them for their father's presents. Suddenly he saw Benjamin standing among his brothers and asked:

"Is this your youngest brother?" And when he heard it was Benjamin he was so deeply moved that he had to go out of the room quickly, so that no one would notice. After a while he grew calm and went back to his brothers; he took the magic cup in his hand, struck against it, listened to the sound and said:

"My magic cup tells me that Reuben is the oldest one among you, therefore he shall be seated at the head of the table. Simeon is the second," and so he went on telling all his brothers their ages and seating each of them in his turn. They then ate and drank with Joseph, but did not yet know that he was their brother.

JOSEPH MAKES HIMSELF KNOWN
TO HIS BROTHERS

As the hour approached when the brothers wished to return home with their newly bought grain, Joseph ordered his people to put the money again into their sacks; but in Benjamin's sack he commanded them to put his magic cup. As the day began to dawn, Joseph's brothers loaded all their goods upon the camels, and set out cheerfully on their way to Canaan.

They had not gone very far when Joseph's servants overtook them and said to them:

"Our master ordered us to hurry after you and to tell you that you have returned good with evil. He invited you to eat with him, entertained you as guests and gave presents to you, but you have robbed him and have taken from him his magic silver cup.

The brothers were very deeply grieved at this and answered only:

"Look in our sacks, and whichever one among us

you find has the cup, that one shall be put to death; and the rest of us you shall make your slaves."

They jumped from their camels, placed their sacks on the earth, and each man opened his own. Joseph's servants searched through the sacks and found the cup in Benjamin's. When the brothers saw this, they tore their clothes in despair. Then they loaded their sacks on the camels again, followed Joseph's servants back into the city and soon appeared once more before Joseph.

"How could you do it?" he asked the men. "Did you not know that a man like me would soon find it out?"

And they answered:

"Master, what shall we say to you? You are just and fair, and we have all done wrong; we are willing to be your servants."

But Joseph said:

"Only the one among you in whose sack the cup was found shall be my servant; the rest of you may go your way in peace."

Then Judah took courage, stepped up to Joseph and said:

"Master, you asked us if we had a father and brothers. We then told you we had an aged father and a very young brother, who is his favorite son because he is the only one left to him by his dead wife Rachel. He loves the boy fervently, and his heart is set upon him. You demanded that we should bring the boy to you. But our father would not give him up until I pledged my own life for my brother. Only then, and with a heavy heart, did he let him go. Now, when we are ready to return home, you wish to hold him here. But if we go back to our father without the boy, he will die of grief. If our brother has stolen, let me bear his punishment, but give him again his freedom."

Then Joseph was no longer able to control himself. He ordered all his servants to leave the room, and when he was left alone with his brothers he cried out to them:

"You told me that your brother Joseph was dead. He is not dead, he lives and you shall see him." And as he noticed how pale the brothers grew with fright, he continued:

"Do you then not recognize your brother Joseph? Look at me very carefully, for I am he whom you sold into Egypt. Listen and I will speak in Hebrew with you. Do not be afraid, but come nearer to me that I may embrace you."

And he embraced all his brothers. Benjamin, however, fell into his arms and wept for joy. Then he gave them beautiful gifts, to Benjamin the most beautiful of all. Finally he turned to Judah and said:

"Judah! I know that you persuaded our brothers to sell me into the land of Egypt. But do not be frightened, for it was God's will, so that I might save the world from famine. Go to our father and bring him here. From now on, you shall live with me in my palaces and gardens, for I am the greatest man in Egypt after Pharaoh."

JACOB'S ARRIVAL IN EGYPT

Joseph sent messengers to Pharaoh with the word that his brothers had come to him out of the land of Canaan. Then Pharaoh wished to see them. And when they went to him, he greeted them graciously and said:

"Go back to the land of Canaan, get your father and all your kinsmen and bring them to Egypt. I will give you land in Egypt, as much of it as you need."

Joseph's brothers were pleased at these words, and they did as Pharaoh had told them. Joseph gave them wagons for the journey, and also food and drink. To his father he sent ten asses, laden with all kinds of precious things out of the land of Egypt; also ten she-asses laden with grain and bread. After that he bade good-bye to his brothers and said to them:

"Do not quarrel along the way, and do not reproach yourselves either, because everything has turned out for the best."

Then the brothers arose and set out for the land

of Canaan. When they arrived at their father's house they told him that Joseph was still alive and that he had become a great lord. At first Jacob was not willing to believe them, but when they repeated Joseph's words to him, and showed him the wagons which Joseph had given them for the journey, and finally when they also delivered his presents to him, then Jacob could no longer doubt. His happiness was indeed great, and he was altogether beside himself with joy; he sobbed and laughed at the same time, he wept happy tears and cried out exultingly:

"My son, my dear son lives! I will see him! I will go to him that I may see him before I die!"

So they lost no time; they loaded their belongings on the wagons, climbed on their camels and went away with all their kindred to the land of Egypt.

On the way they came to Beersheba, and there Jacob offered sacrifices unto the dear Lord and thanked Him for having granted him the blessing of seeing his beloved son once again.

When they were approaching Egypt, Jacob sent his son Judah ahead to inform Joseph of his father's arrival. Then Joseph ordered his carriage, and drove out to meet his father; and when he came to him he fell into his arms and wept a long, long time. But Jacob said:

"Now I can die in peace, since I know that you are alive!"

When they arrived in Egypt, Joseph took his father and five of his brothers and brought them to Pharaoh. And Jacob blessed Pharaoh. The king then asked him:

"How old are you, father?"

And Jacob replied:

"I have lived a hundred and thirty years."

And Pharaoh was well pleased with all of them and he said to Joseph:

"Let them live in my kingdom and give them the best piece of land for their possession. Put the wisest among them, however, in charge of my cattle."

But Joseph's brothers did not want to live among the Egyptians because they were afraid they might learn their evil customs from them.

So Joseph gave them the land of Goshen.

Then Jacob departed with his kindred into the land of Goshen. They were soon entirely familiar with their new home, had many children, and these again had children, and so in time they became a great nation. The Hebrew people later had to suffer many afflictions in the land of Egypt. They were troubled and tormented until Moses set them free. And how all that happened, you will hear in another story.

JACOB'S DEATH

After some time had passed, Jacob became ill and he felt that his end was near. When Joseph learned that his father was dying, he took his two sons Ephraim and Manasseh and hastened to him. And it was told to Jacob that his son Joseph was coming. Then he made a great effort, gathered together all his strength, raised himself up in bed and said:

"Let your sons Ephraim and Manasseh come to my bedside that I may bless them. The God of my fathers, who has delivered me from all evil, bless them, so that they may grow to be great and mighty upon the earth. They shall be as my children. They shall have their share in the land of Israel and each one shall become a tribe for himself."

He begged Joseph to bury him in the land of Israel in the cave of Machpelah and said:

"Do not be angry with me, my son, that I did not lay your mother Rachel to rest in the family burying place. But God did not wish it, and he commanded me to bury her on the way to Bethlehem."

And he told Joseph why God had wanted it so.

After that Jacob had all his sons come to him. They gathered around his bed, and he said to them:

"Reuben, you are my first-born; the right of the first-born belongs to you, you ought to possess the highest honors, and the greatest power. But your nature is unstable, and you shall not have the might that belongs to you.

"Simeon and Levi, your swords are murderous weapons and in your anger you have killed men and trampled animals under foot. I curse your anger because it is too violent. You shall never be together; only divided shall you live among your people.

"Judah, your brothers shall praise you. Your arm shall always be upon the neck of the enemy. Your brothers shall bow down before you, because from you shall the kings of your people come. You are like a young lion; who shall rise up against you? You shall give law and justice to the world, and the nations shall come unto you to learn wisdom of you. Your land shall be rich and fruitful; you shall wash your garments in wine, and your teeth shall be white as milk.

"Issachar and Zebulun, must hold together. Issachar, you shall sit with your books and learn; but Zebulun, you shall engage in business and all the ships which are mine upon the sea shall belong to you. You shall carry on trade, and from the profits you shall support yourself and your brothers."

Thus spoke Jacob to his children, took leave of

them and blessed each in turn. At the end he implored them once again to bury him in the land of Israel and said:

"Bury me in the cave of Machpelah where my father Isaac and my mother Rebekah lie. My grandfather bought the cave from the sons of Heth and I shall rest there near my wife Leah."

And he began to pray:

"Hear, O Israel, our God is the only God."

And his children answered him:

"Amen."

Thereupon he lay down and died.

But since that time the Jews repeat this prayer twice every day. Then their fathers hear it in their graves in the cave of Machpelah, and they know that we still live and keep faith with them.

JACOB'S BURIAL

After the death of Jacob, Joseph went to Pharaoh and told him that his father was dead, and that before his death he had commanded his sons to bury him in the land of Israel. And Pharaoh granted Joseph leave to go to the land of his fathers, that he might bury Jacob there. But the Egyptians wanted to honor Joseph, and did not allow him to depart alone. All the high officials and all the oldest men among the Egyptians arose and accompanied Joseph and his brothers to their native country. On the road to the land of Israel they met Ishmael and Esau who were engaged in war. When these men saw the funeral procession, they took the crowns off their heads and placed them on Jacob's coffin. Thirty-six crowns lay upon the coffin, for thirty-six princes accompanied Jacob to the cave of Machpelah.

When Jacob's sons had arrived in Canaan, they did as their father had commanded them and buried him in the tomb of his fathers, where Abraham and Sarah, Isaac and Rebekah had been laid to rest.

After that they set out again on the road to Egypt. Along the way they passed by the pit into which Joseph had once been thrown by his brothers. Joseph stood beside it for a while, looked down into its depths and said:

"Out of this pit I have been lifted up and have become the ruler for the King of Egypt."

When the brothers heard these words, they thought that Joseph, after their father's death, might want to avenge himself upon them for the suffering which they once had inflicted upon him, and they did not wish to go back with him to Egypt.

But Joseph said to them:

"Do not be afraid. You wanted to treat me wickedly, but God has turned it into good. Therefore do not worry, for I have forgiven you everything and I will take care of you and your children. If ten lights could not put out one light, how could a single light put out all ten?"

Then the brothers hesitated no longer, and went with him back to Egypt.